Lilly

Lilly

Palm Beach, Tropical Glamour, and the Birth of a Fashion Legend

KATHRYN LIVINGSTON

TRADE PAPER
PRESS

Trade Paper Press
An imprint of Turner Publishing Company
Nashville, Tennessee
www.turnerpublishing.com

Cover image: © Davidoff Studios

Cover design: Wendy Mount

Design by Forty-five Degree Design LLC

Library of Congress Cataloging-in-Publication Data:
Livingston, Kathryn, date.
 Lilly : Palm Beach, tropical glamour, and the birth of a fashion legend / Kathryn Livingston.
 p. cm.
 Includes bibliographical references and index.
 ISBN 978-0-470-50160-3 (cloth : alk. paper); ISBN 978-1-118-25866-8 (ebk); ISBN 978-1-118-22034-4 (ebk); ISBN 978-1-118-23375-7 (ebk)
 1. Pulitzer, Lilly. 2. Fashion designers—United States—Biography.
3. Socialites—United States—Biography. 4. Palm Beach (Fla.)—History. I. Title.
 TT505.P85L58 2012
 746.9'2092—dc23 [B]

 2012007300

Printed in the United States of America
10 9 8 7 6 5 4 3 2

To my daughter, Valerie, with her feel for fashion and language

Contents

CONTENTS

Photo gallery begins on page 95.

Acknowledgments

Lilly: Palm Beach, Tropical Glamour, and the Birth of a Fashion Legend could not have happened without the aid and encouragement of a broad cast of caring and contributive individuals. Leading off are the book's two knowledgeable and inspiring editors at Wiley who steered the project through a thicket of challenges. The idea for this book belongs to my original editor, Hana Lane. I would like to express my deepest appreciation for her fine-honed editorial instincts, her sense of style, her vital enthusiasm for the project, and her never-less-than-gracious ways. This book would not have come to life without the active role and focusing skills of my sharp-minded later editor, Thomas W. Miller. I am thankful for his ability to suggest improvements without changing the intended meaning of a point, his tightening of the narrative, and his bringing the book to its final form.

At John Wiley & Sons, I also owe gratitude to assistant editor Jorge Amaral and senior production editor Lisa Burstiner as well

as her team, copyeditor Judith Antonelli and proofreader Rima Weinberg, for their precise reading and skillful sharpening of the text while seeing this book through from manuscript to publication.

I live in fear of not properly thanking the many people who gave freely of their time and memories while I was writing this book. To help me render the particulars of Lilly Pulitzer's life as accurately as possible and to search deeper into the emotional lives of the men and women who surrounded her and influenced the choices she made, a handful of people were particularly essential. Special appreciation goes to my longtime friends Fernanda Kellogg and her husband, Kirk Henckels, both busy New York professionals with strong roots in Palm Beach and personal ties to the Pulitzers, whose astute observations and suggestions provided me with a good starting point. Likewise, I wish to express my gratitude to valued friend Sandy McLanahan, who maintains close links to Palm Beach and generously shared his memories of the spirit of the place as well as of his New England boarding school days, which include recollections about the preppy circle of extraordinary young women who were Lilly's schoolmates at Miss Porter's School in Farmington. I am forever in the debt of Dita Naylor-Leyland, a great-granddaughter of steel industry titan Henry Phipps Jr. She granted me the huge favor of opening windows into the lifestyles of the quietly rich but exceptionally pacesetting intermarried Long Island families who framed Lilly's early years. Dita's cousin Patricia Montgomerie proved to be invaluably encyclopedic about the sporty activities of the horsey set. My appreciative thoughts linger with Nancy Moorland, author of the *The Last Debutante*, who shared with me some illuminating pages from her yet unpublished but most deserving novel about the resplendent social orbit and poignant anxieties of Lilly's mid-century contemporaries who rushed into early marriages. My endless gratitude to two people who have

gone out of their way to patiently assist me with some elusive information: Gonzalo Garcia-Pedroso, with his thoughtful comments and incisive background material about Florida's Cuban families, and Edwina Millington, with her discreet but wittily telling stories about what makes Lilly, her close friend since childhood, so rare and totally unique.

A big thank you goes to the following people who answered questions, told me stories, helped clarify data, directed me to reliable sources, and helped substantiate facts about Palm Beach, fashion, horses, the jet set, Cuban exiles and Lilly Pulitzer Inc. past and present: Dianne Crary, Jon Schotz, Kim Johnson Gross, Mary Phipps, Paul Gachot, Crary Pullen, Margarita Barrera, Fern Tailer, Barbara Cates, Julie Kammerer, Stefane Bartlett, Eve Hatch Holmes, June Weir, and Bob Hardwick. I have relied also on some of my past magazine interviews and conversations regarding topics covered in this book with Rodney Dillard, Marjorie Meek, Mimi Kemble McMakin, Stan Rumbough, Polly Mellen, Jo Leas, Charlie Pepper, David Ober, Agnes Ash, Emilia Fanjul, Bea Cayzer, the late William Hutton III, the late Earl E. T. Smith, the late Whitney Tower, and the late Arthur "Bull" Hancock. Many of these sources were research for an extensive twenty-page article about Palm Beach I did for *Town & Country* magazine with photographer Slim Aarons. A few sources spoke to me on the condition of anonymity.

I have been the beneficiary of fifty years of published materials on Lilly Pulitzer as well as on the many American high-profile high achievers around her—the McKim, Bostwick, Phipps, Grace, Guest, and Pulitzer families. The bulk of my research was done in the archives of the New York Public Library. My endless gratitude is reserved for several of the research divisions of the NYPL, particularly the Science, Industry, and Business Library where I gleaned more of the corporate story behind the Lilly Pulitzer brand; and to the helpful librarians in the Millstein Room of

Genealogical, Biographical, and Local History, who helped to uncover the groundwork that would become the story of Lilly's early life and her family and deep connection to New York City. I also received conscientious assistance from the information-stacked library of New York's Fashion Institute of Technology, the New York Society Library, the New York Historical Society, and the Historical Society of Palm Beach County and Old Westbury Gardens.

Immeasurably helpful were my extraordinary researchers. My writer and archivist daughter, Valerie Livingston, was part of the development of this book from the beginning, adding her library expertise, verbal flair, and fashion savvy. I could not have survived without Kenneth N. Brown, who has been at my side for previous books with his computer brilliance and his exacting and inspired quest for the vast number of factual details needed for the many facets of the narrative. Particularly grateful am I for his scouring of old Florida and Cuban newspapers. I cannot express enough thanks to Kate Giel, whose assistance and support with finding the right photographs was never less than imaginative, energetic, and professional.

I am most appreciative of my family's part in this book. While writing, I often drew on my beautiful Palm Beach memories with my beloved late husband, Russell Forgan, who for a time spent part of every year in a house on Seaspray Avenue and introduced me to the town's special pleasures. Finally, I could not have done without the cheering section, otherwise known as my son, Bret Livingston, and his wife, Patty and their daughters, Walker and Grace. Limitless gratitude and love to all.

CHAPTER 1

It Girl of the Sixties

ON THE PRIVET-ENCLOSED SEAVIEW AVENUE campus of the Palm Beach Day School, a confluence point of the wealthiest families from all over the United States, the popular annual Field Day meet brought a large crowd. The most memorable thing about that April afternoon in 1962 is that everyone had turned up in a uniform—and not just the students.

This was expected of the boys and girls, of course. In they marched—some 350 of them, ranging from kindergarten to ninth grade—lined up in rows of five behind their flag-carrying leaders. They were in their best gym clothes: navy blue polo shirts marked with the prestigious PBDS insignia, crisp white shorts, spotless white socks, and tennis shoes. To differentiate themselves as players on an opposing team, some of the children had donned hunter-green tops over their polo shirts. Their coaches could be spotted scattered

across the school grounds; they too were dressed alike in pastel oxford shirts, with sleeves rolled up, and khaki chino pants.

Altogether unexpected was the sight of all the young mothers whose lives were intertwined by the various athletic contests. From a distance, it looked as though they too were identically dressed. Was it a coincidence or by design? They formed a swaying cavalcade of color on the grassy field as they moved this way and that, following their children from race to race. At closer range, however, it became apparent: every grown-up woman on the scene—without exception—was wearing a vibrantly printed, sleeveless new shift called a Lilly.

Although these cotton dresses were shaped alike, skimming easily over the figure and slightly flared just above the knee for ease of movement, the prints were not all the same. What they had in common was their euphoric effect on the eye. There was a freshness and a shock to this exuberant mix of high-intensity color: sun-drenched hibiscus pinks met with jungle-inspired foliage greens, citrus yellows and oranges with sky-bright blues and ocean-tinted aquamarines.

The clear, bold, and almost childlike print motifs were unique. Swirling with madcap monkeys and butterflies, banana leaves and oversized hothouse blooms, cartoon crocodiles and wittily tilting daiquiri glasses, they had an air of both innocence and sophistication. They articulated something novel and playful about the wild beauty and fun times of contemporary living in warm climates.

There was no getting around it: overnight, Lilly Pulitzer—local girl, fledgling fashion designer—had put the entire female population of this reeflike twelve-mile island, the apex of U.S. luxe resorts, into her Lillys. And suddenly, there she was, in the middle of all the action, in her own pink-and-green Lilly—full of life, tall and tan, earthy and elegant. With an exotically wrapped turban-type headdress, gold gypsy earrings, her voluminous dark hair in a long single braid, and her bare feet—which looked strong enough

to shinny up the nearest coconut tree without any trouble at all—
she looked like a Polynesian queen.

In Palm Beach at this moment, she *was* the queen. Every
woman present pressed in to say a word, shake her hand,
and touch her. Confident and approachable in demeanor, she
was actually a private and reserved person, stunned by the frenzy
and adulation. It was more in character for her to jokingly
shrug off a compliment or modestly downplay an accomplish-
ment. Humor usually served her well when she was faced with an
awkward situation.

"Have I started some weird cult?" flashed through her mind.
Deep down, she was feeling uneasy lately about the hugely
enthusiastic reaction she sometimes elicited from people. Not
knowing what to do, she smiled a shy smile and rolled with the
spontaneity of the moment. She was in her Lilly, they were in
their Lillys, and they were deeply grateful to her for having
invented a uniform for them; it gave them a sense of belonging
and a chance to bask in her special way of life. That way of life
was, in effect, the distillation of a daydream. To many of these
young Palm Beach matrons, the sassy shift with its lush tropical
imagery and effortless air was a fantasy encapsulation of what
they perceived to be the charmed life of Lilly Pulitzer.

"Lilly Pulitzer was the 'It Girl' of the sixties," recalls Fernanda
Kellogg, a vice president at Tiffany & Co. in New York who
grew up in the Florida resort. "She had it all and everybody
in Palm Beach wanted to be like her. She had a sense of style
and a sense of pleasure that was original, natural, and, above all,
young. Sporting a Lilly poolside or at a cocktail party started out
as a youth movement, away from the powder-pink and beige silk
shantungs and serious jewelry of an older, more formal Palm
Beach generation."

Wearing a Lilly also became a sort of wish fulfillment of
being like Lilly. The simple but recognizable shift shape, steadily

multiplying in dozens of color combinations at sought-after Palm Beach clubs like the Everglades and the Bath & Tennis, endowed you with an instant aura of being in the know, aware of all the intricate dos and don'ts of this suddenly exceedingly fashionable and from its beginning highly exclusive enclave.

Palm Beach is where the youthful new occupants of the White House, John F. Kennedy and his family, now regularly wintered. The spotlight had arrived when Kennedy, as president-elect, had spent two and a half months living in his father's Palm Beach villa, writing his inaugural address and setting up his cabinet. In between, he was unwinding from what had been a rigorous political campaign. He was seen sailing on the *Honey Fitz*, Christmas shopping on Worth Avenue with his children, Caroline and John John, and attending Christmas Eve Mass with the future First Lady, who looked lovely in her white gloves and tiny mantilla of frosty lace.

After the inauguration ceremony in Washington, which many in the media still consider the best political celebration of the twentieth century—a "gilt-edged, mink-lined, silk-hatted, 10-gallon, 100-proof" party, as a *Washington Post* cub reporter named Tom Wolfe summed it up at the time—all of the Kennedy comings and goings in quietly wealthy Palm Beach were suddenly dazzlingly recorded in press photographs and TV news segments.

Lilly had been a childhood friend of Jacqueline Kennedy. When Jackie and little Caroline were later photographed in matching Lillys, both the cotton shift and the Pulitzer name gained national attention from their association with the promise and style of the young administration.

Emulating Lilly's style back in Palm Beach implied being part of her inner circle and having what she had: that special way of life. And in the early 1960s, Lilly appeared to have everything that

a woman, especially an American woman, could want. Well-born and good-looking, she had a rich and glamorous husband who flew his own private plane, three children, and an attractive house on Lake Worth, which was not a lake at all but an inlet of the Atlantic Ocean. She and her husband were still in their twenties, and there among the tangled banyan trees the young couple pioneered a new kind of lifestyle. It was informal, embracing the pleasures of nature—a touch jungly and decidedly barefoot.

The turn-of-the-century clapboard house was a place to which everyone wanted to go: full of children, dogs, music, energy, and fun. Inside, modern comfort met a carefree mix of tropical and Victorian. Someone always knew how to pluck the strings of a guitar, dance the limbo, or do the twist. The couple didn't need servants to slash open a pineapple, slice up a mango, mash an avocado into guacamole, or crack open the claw of a South Florida blue crab for a chilled seafood salad. Lilly and her husband threw casual dinner parties in their big bright kitchen that could seat more than thirty people. They put guests to work chopping and stirring. After dinner, they used the empty champagne bottles to slosh water on the tile floor, making it slippery for dancing that sometimes went on until four in the morning.

Although they stayed away from the resort's glittering charity balls, languorous country club lunches, and long afternoons on the golf course, Lilly and her husband had a *civilized* barefoot life. And it was the talk of the town. "One of the first things I saw in Palm Beach was the Pulitzers and a few friends having a quiet drink in the stern of their yacht," remembers a woman who arrived at the resort in 1961. "It was tied up at the dock, and I was crossing the Royal Palm Bridge, and the evening sun was coming across Lake Worth, and I thought, 'There are the most attractive people I have ever seen.'"

Lilly McKim Pulitzer had started coming to Palm Beach when she was a little girl. Her mother had divorced Lilly's father and remarried; she was now Mrs. Ogden Phipps, and if one had to pick a name that stood for the leading family of Palm Beach in those days, *Phipps* would have been it. Members of this East Coast clan had the largest real estate holdings not only on the island but also throughout the state of Florida. They lived in quiet luxury and knew exactly how to avoid publicity or how to use it to advance their national prominence when it involved their horses, their philanthropies, and their achievements.

Either way, the distinguishing Phipps characteristic was to do everything better than anyone else did. Perhaps the most obvious testament to the Phipps family's position of privilege was that Michael Phipps—the vice president of the family's Bessemer Trust, a permanent resident of Palm Beach, and Lilly's stepuncle—was given the only exception to the town law prohibiting helicopters from taking off from and landing on the island.

Lilly's husband, Herbert "Peter" Pulitzer Jr., also came from a family with immense power and an instantly recognizable name. His grandfather founded the *St. Louis Post-Dispatch*, made the *New York World* into the largest-circulation newspaper in the United States, and established the Pulitzer Prize. Peter was an entrepreneur in his own right. He cultivated citrus trees and had developed the extensive four-hundred-acre Pulitzer Groves north of Palm Beach in the still relatively wild inland country near Lake Okeechobee, where not only alligators, venomous snakes, red fire ants, and Florida panthers, but even the vegetation of spikelet-tipped sandbur and dagger-shaped, serrated-leafed saw palmetto could bite you back if you didn't watch your step.

On the whole, longtime resort regulars and self-appointed social arbiters viewed Lilly and Peter as a couple of amusing

exotics: nonconformist and somewhat rebellious, especially whenever they were seen walking barefoot with their pet rhesus monkey, Gooney, along the immaculately groomed residential streets with turquoise swimming pools behind their mansion gates. They were different from most of their Ivy League school peers, and with their darkly browned bodies and leggy grace, they evoked comparisons to Tarzan and Jane.

One thing that made them different was that they stayed in Palm Beach—very much a seasonal resort—during the scorching summer months. More notably, they both worked. That was still quite unusual in the early 1960s in this privileged home of the so-called idle rich. Lilly was already recognized as a successful young tycoon with a busy boutique in town and, it was whispered, on the brink of becoming a national fashion star.

Lilly's life seemed almost too good to be true. But the woman who has everything has everything to lose. Already Lilly had known both good fortune and calamity and grief. She was always good at keeping her troubles hidden or, at least, holding her cards close to the chest. She was already having occasional tremulous feelings about the effect that celebrity might have on her idyllic personal life, her "perfect marriage," and her beautiful and adored children.

What no one was aware of in 1962, and few people know even now, is that Lilly's uplifting fashion enterprise was born of a debilitating emotional crisis. After giving birth to her third child in four years, Lilly fell into a postpartum depression. When she left the psychiatric clinic four months later, her doctor softly patted her on the shoulder. "Keep busy" was his wise parting advice.

No one could have guessed that what began as a snob uniform in Palm Beach would soon travel to points north, become a much-copied national fashion craze, and eventually be exhibited by the

curators of the Smithsonian Institution as an American classic. And after its decline, no American fashion house that had to close down because of its dimming luster with the public has ever made it back and achieved the kind of triumphant second life as the never-forgotten Lilly Pulitzer brand did in the twenty-first century. Five decades later, the flamboyantly printed shift, still true to Lilly's original vision of the sensual ease of the tropics, is the basis of a multimillion-dollar fashion empire, invigorated by a third generation's demand for it.

CHAPTER 2

The Healing Properties of Florida Orange Juice

ILLY'S KNACK FOR HAVING FUN AND HER HABIT OF leaning toward the sunny side of life abruptly abandoned her in 1957. Suddenly, a few weeks after delivering her third child, Liza, in June, she fell silent. She was unable to speak. She tried to form words, but no sound would escape from her lips, and she was unwilling or incapable of writing down anything. Her powers of concentration and her means of communicating with people seemed impaired. She lacked the energy to carry out the day-to-day tasks of family life.

Those closest to her were told by the doctor that she had suffered a nervous collapse. The consensus was that she should return to New York, where she was originally from, and enter a hospital where she would receive expert analysis and care.

Years later, when close friends would broach the subject and press her about what had happened, Lilly would say

that she had been overwhelmed by a mixture of exhaustion, isolation, and boredom. But a feeling of inadequacy finally overtook her. And with that came guilt and hopelessness. Although she was excited and felt blessed to have each of her three children and, in her words, "loved my kids more than life itself," the thought of taking care of one more baby created a tremendous fear that she did not have the inner wherewithal to cope, to give enough to all three. Knowing the extraordinary degree of attention the new infant would require, Lilly was terrified of shortchanging her firstborn son, Peter, who was barely three years old at that time, and her daughter Minnie, who had celebrated her first birthday just weeks before Liza arrived.

Lilly had always felt a sadness once the season in Palm Beach was over and her friends left for their homes up north. The island population dropped to a ghostly few thousand residents. And the hushed, uneventful off-season lasted for an interminably long eight months. "Palm Beach was different in those days," she confided to writer Jay Mulvaney. In the book she co-authored with him, regarding entertaining, she reminisced, "Oh, in the summer it was dead. D-E-A-D." All the street lamps would be removed, extra sand would cover all the roads and less than a handful of stores would stay open all year round.

Lilly often felt lonely. She missed the people she had known all her life, the revved-up New York tempo she had grown up with, and the perpetual involvement in worthwhile civic or sports activity pursued by her relatives on Long Island. Although she had been vacationing in Palm Beach during the high social season since childhood, she was basically a stranger to the year-round tropics. The endless blazing sun, the monotonous flatness of the land, and the relentless Florida humidity made her lazy and logy. Looking at the unoccupied locked houses, their windows sealed up with sheets of metal as protection from the hurricanes that usually arrived in the late summer, she felt empty.

Above all, she was anguished by a vague longing for something undefined from her husband. She was conscious that the terrain of her marriage was somehow shifting under her feet. The more worried and melancholy she became, the less she was in harmony with Peter's easygoing, go-getting temperament.

Lilly was under twenty-one, when she married him. Before that, she "never thought about what marriage was . . . it was just my next adventure," she was quoted in *Vanity Fair.* In an article in *W* magazine, she told interviewer Lorna Koski, "I was not the most mature kid on the block. . . . I wasn't up to it. . . . My marriage was driving me crazy . . . and I did not want to admit that, even to myself."

In the early fall of 1957, Lilly entered a psychiatric clinic north of New York City, the Westchester branch of Payne Whitney, now part of the Weill Cornell Medical Center of New York–Presbyterian Hospital. Surrounded by flower gardens and rolling greenery, the place was in those days euphemistically referred to as Bloomingdale's. This was because so many fashionable young women from Manhattan's high-strung, high-maintenance Upper East Side were treated there for nervous breakdowns.

In a *New Yorker* profile by Larissa MacFarquhar in September 2000, Lilly recalled the months she spent in the clinic in analysis and therapy: "I had a great time. It was like going back to boarding school—very regimented." Her occupational therapy often consisted of sketching. One of her longtime friends, who was once a fashion editor in New York, had a chance to glimpse some of these old drawings, which Lilly had saved in a hardcover folder held together by a grosgrain ribbon. In this friend's opinion, "Lilly could have become an artist. No detail escaped her. She had a total command of proportion and scale and color."

Toward the end of her hospital stay, the doctor said to Lilly, "There is nothing wrong with you; you just need something to do. You're not happy because you're not doing anything."

"But I don't know how to do anything," Lilly answered. "I'd always had everything done for me, always had my nanny and my mummy making up my mind for me." In several magazine interviews over the years she bemoaned the fact that until her marriage she never had a responsibility in her life, quipping self-deprecatingly: "My pea-brain wasn't up to it."

"You've got to go out and find something to do," he insisted.

The willingness to be happy trickled back slowly, in small, gradual doses over a period of four months. Once she had become more like her former cheerful self, her determination to stay healthy was quick and unshakable.

"I followed the doctor's advice and came out of the hospital a lot stronger, and I haven't stopped since," she said years later in the interview with Lorna Koski, in *W*. After months of counseling during her treatment and recovery, she added, "I became much more assertive."

Lilly made a decision to start her own business and she needed to implement her resolve right away. She had ample reason to do so. The situation was fragile, the stakes immense. Having made many impulsive, reckless decisions in the past, always wanting to do things as she pleased, she now could not afford to make a false step. Lilly had always been a renegade, but she claimed that she did not set out to be an unusual person or to be different. "I just wanted to do things my way," she told Koski.

When she returned to Florida, her friends noticed that she was still a bit more quiet and subdued than she had been before her illness. She was grateful that Peter had been such an involved and loving father to young Peter, Minnie, and Liza during her absence. He had help, of course, from several loyal and seasoned nannies long in Lilly's family's employment. And since Lilly had always been close to her own nannies during her formative years, she was less reluctant than most young mothers would be today to entrust children to nannies, because the ones

she knew had well-trained hands and reliably conscientious hearts. "As a child, I was always being told not to be so familiar with the staff. But I couldn't help it," she reflected in a 2003 *Vanity Fair* interview with Laura Jacobs. "I was close to them, spent a lot of time with them, we were friends." Actually, she had had no choice but to rely on these women when she was hospitalized— or according to several friends, now bluntly refers to that time as "when I went off to the nuthouse"—especially since it was initially difficult to estimate the seriousness of her illness and gauge the duration of time she would need to be away from her children.

She knew the doctor was right about the dangers of idleness and how urgent it was to find something useful to do. But what could she do? Unlike most of her schoolmates from Chapin, New York's prestigious private girls' school, and Miss Porter's School in Connecticut, she had not benefited from the cultural riches or the applicable professional knowledge of a four-year liberal arts college. She did not even attend one of those finishing-school- type two-year junior colleges, which was the custom at the time for many well-off young women who were simply expected to marry and not pursue a career.

Lilly had been enrolled at Finch College in New York City, but before the first semester was over she had already quit. She packed it all in and went off "to do something real," according to one of her girlhood friends from Long Island. Since she had ridden horses all of her life, what appealed to her was the Frontier Nursing Service.

The Frontier Nursing Service was started in Leslie County, Kentucky, by Mary Breckinridge in 1925 and run by her until her death in 1965. An early crusader for prenatal care among the American rural poor, Breckinridge focused her work on the vast forested areas of eastern Kentucky, where in the 1920s some ten thousand people lived tucked away in the mountains, often sixty miles in any direction from a paved road or a physician. In her

field studies during the first half of the twentieth century, Breckinridge covered approximately seven hundred miles of desolate back country, where rough-hewn shacks and family log cabins were reachable only on horseback or with mule teams—for years the only modes of travel in the area. Breckinridge found that the women in Leslie, Clay, Perry, and Harlan Counties gave birth to an average of nine children each and were attended primarily by self-taught midwives. The region had exceptionally high maternal and infant death rates.

When Lily decided to join Breckinridge's field of operations, she did so more out of rebellion against the restrictive choices she had been born and bred to make than out of a fervent desire to improve the lives of people less fortunate than herself. She had always liked animals, and grooming and caring for horses and mules were part of the job. She would frequently ride a mule or a horse through the woodsy Kentucky hills, delivering medicine and supplies to needy mothers and newborn babies in remote outposts.

Sometimes Lilly would be asked to lend a hand in home births. At other times she served as an assistant nurse-midwife in the delivery room of the Mary Breckinridge Hospital, which had just been built at the top of Thousandsticks Mountain by the time Lilly arrived in 1949. Fifteen mule teams had pulled the cement and plaster up former footpaths and horse trails of the still mostly undeveloped terrain.

Statistics taken after every thousand births and tabulated over the years by the Metropolitan Life Insurance Company show that the work of the Frontier Nursing Service dramatically improved the quality of life in the region. This health-care system resulted in an almost immediate decrease in infant mortality. The weights of newborn babies went up and the death rates of mothers went down.

During Lilly's stay in Kentucky, another major challenge in this mountainous hinterland was communication. Mail usually came

once a day, but phone service was still pretty unreliable. Young volunteers like Lilly, recruited by Breckinridge from philanthropic-minded families, were sometimes also used as couriers, carrying news and information along with supplies in their saddles between the hospital and the more far-flung clinical stations. These young women from wealthy families arrived seeking adventure and an opportunity to serve, but the rugged existence was a far cry from the glamorous lives some of them were accustomed to.

Soon after her arrival in Kentucky from New York, Lilly learned that she was part of something important that would contribute to many families' lives, but as the months wore on, she also increasingly felt cut off from the outside world. She longed to be able to share her thoughts with the many friends and confidantes—especially her sisters—whom she had left behind. Experimenting further in the health-care area, which she found rewarding, but wanting to get back to New York, Lilly became a nurse's aide at the Veterans Hospital in the Bronx. "I liked it. Just giving time," she said about these two medical work experiences to Laura Jacobs in a July 2003 article in *Vanity Fair*.

Eight years later, in 1957, coming home from a hospital stay herself, Lilly had arrived at another crossroad. Ever true to herself, she again chose the unconventional path.

Peter Pulitzer often toiled in the mud alongside members of the Seminole tribe near his Indian River citrus groves, especially when the roots of the orange trees had to be flooded with warm water to protect them from a freeze on the way. He was a great believer in the emotional rewards of physical exertion. He concurred with the New York doctor and wholeheartedly supported Lilly's resolve never again to allow herself to feel the sluggishness and despair that made it difficult for her to navigate daily life.

No doubt Peter fully participated in the discussion when the idea was hatched of how Lilly could most meaningfully and purposefully occupy herself. What she decided to do was so unexpected, yet so logical and simple, that when other Palm Beach women heard about it, they laughed or said they would have fainted at the thought of doing it themselves. Lilly started selling oranges and grapefruit from her husband's groves.

The Indian River Citrus District, where Peter's orchards were located, produces some of the finest oranges and grapefruit in the world. Indian River grapefruit has a distinctive sweetness and juiciness that, according to the growers and packers of the region, cannot be found anywhere else on earth. Like the appellations in wine country—for example, the Russian River region in California—the label is controlled and has a coveted cachet. The Indian River Citrus League, organized in 1931, annually presents hall of fame awards for excellence in the upkeep of quality produce and citrus products. It is a growers' association that represents orchards from Daytona to West Palm Beach. The fertile river-coursed terrain extends inland across several of Florida's twenty different ecosystems—such as sand hills, scrub, mangrove shoals, swamp, tropical hammock, and pine forests—between the Atlantic Ocean and several lakes, the largest of which is Okeechobee.

Oranges are not native to Florida. The fruit is a hybrid of ancient origin, but its seeds most likely arrived from New Orleans around 1872, when many orange groves were established in the state by grafting sweet orange onto sour orange rootstocks. Oranges cannot be artificially ripened and must be mature when picked. Florida laws forbid harvesting immature fruit for human consumption. The Indian River area of Florida is known for the high quality of its orange juice, which is frequently sold fresh. Unlike Brazil, which exports 99 percent of its orange juice, 90 percent of Florida orange juice is consumed in the United States.

Lilly began her enterprise the way encyclopedia salesmen or political canvassers did in the 1950s: by going door-to-door. Absolute freshness and the high-quality Indian River trademark were her selling points. Most mornings, Peter would fly up to Fort Pierce at daybreak in his seaplane and return with bags full of freshly picked oranges grown at his grove. Then Lilly would drive around to the back doors of all the big Palm Beach houses—which she was otherwise used to entering through the front doors—and sell the fruit out of the back seat of the family station wagon.

"I got to know every cook, every butler, every maid in Palm Beach," she recalled in a 1994 interview in the South Florida *Sun Sentinel.* "I had a wonderful time and I made $30,000 in a couple of months."

Soon she graduated to selling gift boxes of oranges and grapefruit. This became such a success that Peter would no longer just give her oranges but would make her pay for them. He urged her to open a shop where she could attractively display crates and baskets and book a lot more orders. But Lilly came up with what she considered a better business plan.

By this time both her work ethic and her intuitive eco-consciousness kicked in. She disliked waste. Visual perfectionist that she was, she realized that it would always be difficult to sell an orange that was in any way discolored, bruised, or misshapen. However, juicing some of these perfectly ripe and delicious oranges could turn a potential loss into a profit. Furthermore, squeezing the fruit and quenching the thirst of her many friends could be made into a marvelous fun activity: a party.

Lilly always loved a good time. How could she be more usefully engaged than by gathering up some of the overabundant harvest from her husband's citrus groves and opening a delightful little refreshment stand near the corner of Worth Avenue, the main shopping street in Palm Beach?

Lilly had stumbled onto an idea that would change her life.

CHAPTER 3

Barefoot on Worth Avenue

S ETTING UP A HUMBLE LITTLE ORANGE JUICE STALL just off Worth Avenue, one of the most opulent shopping streets on earth, was certainly an offbeat choice. Formally lined on both sides by tall, stately, gently swaying royal palms and haughty store facades of white marble and pink coral, the avenue was a showcase for the costliest things of this world. Scottish cashmeres, exotic mother-of-pearl inlaid cabinets from Syria, Louis XV consoles and ormolu clocks, thick monogrammed towels and sheets, fancy engraved stationery, Florentine-style bound books, French toy soldiers, English riding boots, haute couture gowns, and glittering necklaces of sapphires, emeralds, rubies, and diamonds competed for attention from the nation's richest strollers and browsers. Lilly's latest entrepreneurial effort was akin to setting up a lemonade stand on Milan's Via Montenapoleone or Beverly Hills's Rodeo Drive.

On the first morning of her new adventure, there was Lilly, barefoot as always. She had on short shorts and a white linen blouse, was wearing no makeup, and had her hair in pigtails. She looked rather Native American—which she was often mistaken for, such as when she had arrived shoeless with baby Peter strapped to her back one day at the pediatrician's office and heard the receptionist announce to the doctor, "There's an Indian out here, and she says she has an appointment."

Lilly was busily arranging napkins and cups around a small vase of flowers and a big industrial-size chrome juicer, trying to make her temporary bar look inviting. She was relieved to see the old mud-streaked station wagon pull up, and she began lifting out crates and bag after bag of oranges freshly picked and personally flown down from Fort Pierce by her husband in his two-seater seaplane. He had already splashed down twice earlier that morning because the plane had room for only a limited amount of fruit.

Curious window shoppers as well as resort regulars rolling by in their Bentleys and Rolls-Royces stopped to see what was going on. They were amused to see the daughter of one of the town's pedigreed old-line families madly juicing oranges on a street corner. Because of Lilly's spirited attitude and her lineage, people found this, like her previous eccentricities, rather enchanting.

Lilly was most definitely considered Palm Beach royalty. Ever since she was six, when her mother had married Ogden Phipps, a Harvard-educated financier, court tennis champion and pillar of New York horse racing, Lilly had spent every winter on this exclusive moated island. People were familiar with the Phipps family's breathtaking houses, each with a private beach, on a huge tract of land north of the Breakers Hotel, such as the Casa Bendita, designed in lavish Mediterranean style by Addison

Mizner with its colonnades, patios, loggias, and stairs open to the tropical breezes.

The Phippses' large gardens were full of butterfly orchids and gardenias and the walls spilled over with bougainvillea and alamander. They often had two swimming pools at one house, half of one pool in the garden and the other half inside the house, and another larger pool near the tennis court, made of coral with sculptured stone heads with mouths that gushed water. Then there was the Phippses' houseboat, the *Seminole*, which would ply the waters off the Florida Keys with all of the grandchildren aboard and proudly return from these outings displaying giant tarpons, sailfish, and other catch of the day.

For the Phipps family, the annual trip down to Florida was made by private train from one of Long Island's great estates, where little girls wore pinafores of Irish lace and little boys dressed in suits ordered from London tailors. There was a private railroad car for the immediate family and the children's nannies, another car for all of their various servants, and still another for their pets and polo ponies.

Peggie Phipps Boegner, Ogden Phipps's first cousin, who had also since girlhood wintered in Palm Beach, at her father Jay Phipps's Casa Bendita, was once asked by her oldest grandson in a rather shocked voice, "Grandma, didn't you ever think of your grandfather, who worked so hard to give you all these luxuries?" She said that she had to answer, "No, I don't think I ever did." But she considered the question later and concluded, "We were the third generation living in an affluent era. Most of our friends seemed rich or rich enough, and of course all our aunts and uncles had places just like ours."

The Phippses made their fortune during the Gilded Age with Andrew Carnegie. Over the years the family was less conspicuous to the general public than were other wealthy American dynasties, like the du Ponts and the Fords, whose inventions in synthetic

fibers and automobiles, changed the American landscape and who owned colossal corporations bearing their names, or the Mellons and the Rockefellers, who initiated monumental charitable foundations and channeled millions into art museums and scientific institutions named after them. The Phipps family gained enormous social cachet from its association with a rich man's sport. That thoroughbred racing had captured the public's fancy and that the Phippses' cousins, the Guests, excelled at polo and were related to Winston Churchill and the Duke of Marlborough added considerably to the Phippses' patrician aura. They were also clannish and private, happiest amongst their many cousins, preferring swimming, playing games, putting on children's plays and entertaining at home rather than going to clubs or frequenting restaurants. According to Peggie Phipps Boegner, "With the exception of Michael and Molly [Ogden's first cousin and his English-born wife, who in the 1950s decided to build a house in Palm Beach, while buying huge tracts of ranch land for breeding cattle about an hour away by helicopter, before land prices in the region soared], none of us ever became part of the Palm Beach scene."

Yet they periodically made headlines. Amy Phipps Guest, Ogden's aunt, a backer of aviator Amelia Earhart's historic flight, opened her spectacular oceanfront estate, Villa Artemis, during World War II to the U.S. Navy and let the government turn it into a convalescent home for wounded sailors. This is the lavish Palm Beach villa depicted in the photograph on the cover of Slim Aarons's book, *Once upon a Time*, with ice-blond society trendsetter C. Z. Guest, Amy's daughter-in-law, dressed in white against the glorious blue swimming pool.

Ogden Phipps's colossally rich Hudson Valley cousin, Ogden L. Mills, became Herbert Hoover's secretary of the treasury in 1932. Another well-known Phipps cousin, African gamesman and crusading early conservationist Bradley Martin, published his book on the plight of the savanna's many endangered species.

There is an irony in the fact that Lilly Pulitzer launched what would become an iconic fashion label by standing shoeless on a street corner and that her fame would rest on a little dress that would epitomize the barefoot pleasures of the privileged life, what she likes to call "affluence at ease." For what made the enjoyment of considerable wealth possible for the subsequent generations of the Phipps clan was the iron work ethic of steel master Henry Phipps Jr. (1839–1934), Ogden's grandfather, the publicity-shy business partner of nineteenth-century industrial giant Andrew Carnegie.

After the Civil War, when raw materials were wrested from the earth to build railroads, bridges, and skyscrapers, it was from a place called Barefoot Square that Henry Jr. pulled himself out of poverty. One of the most downtrodden sections of Allegheny City (today part of Pittsburgh), Barefoot Square got its name because it was so drab and dusty. It was where new immigrants from the British Isles came, seeking to improve their economic lot, living crowded together in the back rooms of cobbler stores and sweatshops.

Henry Jr. was the third of four children of emigrants from Shropshire, England. His parents originally settled in Philadelphia, where Henry was born, and his father supported the family by stitching, gluing, hammering, and selling shoes from the back of a horse-drawn cart. In 1845, Henry Sr. and his wife, Hannah, decided to move farther west in Pennsylvania. They put down roots in Barefoot Square, where their neighbors were William and Margaret Carnegie, who had two sons, Andrew and Tom. Living next door to one another, the three Phipps brothers (John, William, and Henry Jr.), and the two Carnegie boys played together as children and formed close ties as young men while they debated the issues of the day and determined to escape the hard life in Barefoot Square.

The Phipps brothers vowed among themselves to avoid at all costs confinement to the cobbler's bench. Henry Jr. assisted his father at the despised family trade, as his brothers had done before him, until he left school at age fourteen. Then he worked for three years as an apprentice in a jeweler's shop, earning $1.25 a week. "I went to the office before seven in the morning," he recalled in a letter to his son Jay years later. "In the winter I rose in the dark in an unwarmed house, in a room where the water often froze in the pitcher. A long day's duties found me at home in the evening glad to be with my dear Father & Mother, Brothers and Sister. No thought of pleasure, save as it was found in the discharge of duty."

A somber-faced young man who looked rather like the young Henry Fonda, Henry Phipps Jr. soon doubled his apprentice wages, but by 1856 he was impatient to move up into Pittsburgh's burgeoning business world. He was particularly inspired by a letter from his brother John, who was Andrew Carnegie's best friend and intended future partner in embarking on an ambitious foray into what he called "the churning seas of 19th century industry."

John wrote to Henry that year, "Life was not given to us to be frittered away in dreamy Indolence. There is room enough in this great world for all of us to exercise our talents and energy. So much is there to be learnt, so much work to perform, that I frequently think the span of Existence is scarcely long enough to accomplish it. . . . Don't you think the star of the Phipps family is in the ascendant?"

John did not live to see his dream realized. Shortly after writing this, he was killed in a fall from a horse. Andrew Carnegie kept an eye on his late friend's younger brother. In his autobiography, Carnegie wrote of Henry Jr. that he "was several years my junior, but he had not failed to attract my attention as a bright, clever lad . . . energetic and willing. . . . There was no holding back a boy like that."

To illustrate his point, Carnegie recounted an incident that particularly impressed him. One day Henry Jr. asked his brother John for a quarter. John sensed that Henry had an important use for it and handed him a shiny quarter without question. The next morning this advertisement appeared in the *Pittsburgh Dispatch*: "A willing boy wishes work." The ad caught the attention of the firm of Dilworth and Bidwell, a dealer in iron and railroad spikes. Henry was hired as an errand boy. He enrolled in night school to take courses in accounting, which he excelled in, and five years later, at the age of twenty-two, he was named the firm's bookkeeper and offered a partnership.

His reputation as a first-rate bookkeeper rapidly spread among the coterie of ambitious young men formerly of Barefoot Square, some of whom were beginning to succeed. Soon he was offered a second job (to which he walked three miles each night) by another ironworks company that manufactured railroad equipment. Here too he became a partner, and by 1865, the Klopman and Phipps Company merged with Andrew Carnegie's Cyclops Iron Company to form the Union Iron Mills, which at this time of tremendous expansion in the United States (1886) was renamed Carnegie, Phipps. In 1892 it became the mighty Carnegie Steel Company.

Always adept at bookkeeping, Henry Jr. by this time had an exceptional grasp of finance. As treasurer of the Carnegie Steel Company, he worked a sixty-hour week. With his innate frugality, he scrutinized all matters of credit, loans, discounts, and payroll to ensure the highest return on the dollar. His thrift and acumen with numbers were invaluable to the vociferous and more outgoing Andrew Carnegie during the company's early years. When cash was scarce, Phipps had a masterful ability to float checks so that profit could be poured back into the fledgling firm's coffers.

"No one could keep a check longer in the air," it was whispered about him among his rivals during the rapid growth of the Carnegie steel empire. Phipps had a genius for making the same

dollar do many jobs. He could be persuasive as he went from bank to bank along Pittsburgh's Wood Street, insisting that it would be to the financial institution's advantage to waive payment for a few more days, providing capital for Carnegie when it was needed. Phipps also applied his tightwad talents to the manufacturing end of the business. By recycling waste—flue cinder, a by-product of the blast furnace, plus the chips and shavings thrown off as the hot metal passed through the rollers of the steel mill—Carnegie Steel gained tremendous advantage over its competitors.

After Frick Coke Works became aligned with Carnegie Steel in 1881, Andrew Carnegie especially valued Henry Jr. as a conciliator during the many explosive personal conflicts between himself and another Pittsburgh industrial titan, Henry Clay Frick. Phipps hated being in the middle of these periodic combustions of egos, and several times he came close to resigning. "Troubles unnumbered—unending, life too short, the game not worth the candle," Phipps wrote to Carnegie. At times like that, Carnegie accepted Phipps's philosophical words with the wisdom of experience and trust in the history of give-and-take with his "old pard," as he referred to Henry. He was comforted at the thought of their long relationship, through which each of them had prospered in an extraordinary way.

Phipps recognized that Frick's impressive leadership was necessary for restructuring Carnegie Steel's various interests into a powerful unified whole. Phipps fully endorsed Frick's contributions to the business, which ensured that every aspect of steelmaking, from mining the iron ore to rolling the steel, could be performed by the same company. What this meant was that all profits poured straight into the company.

A moving force in the world of the American steel industry, Henry Jr. pops up only briefly, in a few lines here and there, in the many biographies written about Carnegie and Frick. "Grandpa

always avoided publicity," maintained Peggie Phipps Boegner in *Halcyon Days*. Henry Jr. remained by choice a private person, unlike the other great industrialists of his age, especially Carnegie, whose name is on one of the world's most renowned concert halls, and Frick, whose former home on Fifth Avenue and art acquisitions form one of New York City's most exquisite museums, the Frick Collection. Henry paid dearly for his insistence on privacy, according to Boegner, "by often being misunderstood while alive and all but forgotten after his death."

For example, by the 1880s Phipps had begun making sizable donations, but "only to causes he believed just," Boegner qualified. His earliest gifts to the city of Pittsburgh—twenty-five thousand dollars to the public library and ever larger sums for public parks, playgrounds, and baths—were met with outrage because he stipulated that all these places be kept open on Sunday. The city's ministry denounced him for desecrating the traditions of the "Lord's day."

When the stormy Frick-Carnegie relationship finally broke in public, Phipps was on Frick's side. Phipps was caught between his principles and his loyalty to Carnegie, with whom he had worked shoulder to shoulder and whose mistrust he had never incurred. He voiced his opinion directly to Carnegie, a man accustomed to having his own way, and suffered through the combat quietly while scrupulously safeguarding appearances. The conflict was settled out of court in 1900, but it set the stage for the eventual selling of the newly reorganized and renamed Carnegie Company to be bought by J. P. Morgan's U.S. Steel Corporation for a then amazing $480 million.

The cobbler's son from Barefoot Square was the second largest stockholder in the Carnegie Company, next to only Andrew Carnegie. Phipps was a multimillionaire, but he was shy and retiring by nature. He had married late, a woman much younger than he named Annie Childs Shaffer, who was not rich and for

whom it was a big adjustment to handle servants. Held back by their backgrounds of poverty and strict Victorian morality, Phipps and his wife never fully enjoyed the social milieu into which their wealth thrust them.

However, his letters written to the second generation of Phippses show that his five children—Amy (Mrs. Frederick E. Guest), John S. (known as Jay), Helen (Mrs. Bradley Martin), Henry Carnegie Phipps (known as Hal or H.C.), and Howard—were already comfortable within the upper echelon of American society. "Don't play polo or buy polo ponies," Henry Jr. cautioned his oldest son, Jay. Polo in the 1920s was considered the ultimate aristocratic sport in the United States, especially as played in Westbury, Long Island. It was also the costliest. Despite this admonition, Jay became the owner of the best string of polo ponies on Long Island. But it would be the subsequent generations who would most fully enjoy the world that these men and women had created for them.

Social historian Cleveland Amory once observed that traditionally it is the fourth generation in American families built on great fortunes that tends to show a rebellious impulse typical of the rich hippies of the 1960s. Lilly's stepfather, Ogden, was the son of Henry Carnegie Phipps, one of Henry Jr.'s sons. As Ogden's stepdaughter and therefore the equivalent of the fourth generation in a family of achievers, Lilly was surrounded during most of her formative years by people who looked down on indolence and who were competitive, enterprising, and perpetually doing things—be that increasing their wealth, doing charity work, or pursuing sports. As someone driven since childhood by the need to do something worthwhile, Lilly heartily embraced the dichotomy between the working-class chores of a curbside citrus juicer with the élan and assurance of one who indisputably belongs to high society.

To some extent this wish to please mutually contradictory groups had always been part of her existence. It kicked in while she was growing up close to the cooks and gardeners in her homes, during her nurse's aide stint among the disadvantaged in the rugged Kentucky hills, and certainly during the equalizing routines of her painful stay among a diversity of patients at the psychiatric clinic.

Lilly found her orange juice stand a totally thrilling new endeavor. In late 1958, barefoot Lilly Pulitzer—standing near Worth Avenue for hours, cutting open and squeezing orange after orange, the juice sometimes running down her arms and the acid burning into the paper cuts she had acquired while unpacking the cartons of fruit—was not unlike the young Henry Phipps Jr. waking each dawn for the pleasure "found in the discharge of duty." Without knowing it, Lilly was embarking on a career that would become legend.

The cooling tangy drinks and their sweet natural vendor became an instant hit. But Lilly soon found that the work was incredibly messy. There was all that orange juice and grapefruit pulp, not to mention the perspiration worked up bending, pressing, and reaching all day in the oppressive heat, which ruined all of her nicely ironed blouses, shorts, skirts, and pants. She needed to find something that wouldn't show all those messy stains.

She decided to design a work uniform for herself—something that looked already splattered with juice, made of a lively print that had orange, yellow, green, and pink in its color scheme. So she picked up some cheap, brightly colored fabric at the five-and-dime and asked a favorite family seamstress, an elderly woman from Switzerland who had in the past sewn things for her because she was often heard complaining to family members about how she hated shopping and didn't like clothes, to make her a dress. Lilly didn't provide a dress pattern for the seamstress, but she told her she wanted the easiest, coolest, most unencumbered shape imaginable,

sort of a shift or a "little nothing" dress. "Little nothing," a favorite fashion copywriters' phrase of the sixties that began turning up in the pages of *Harper's Bazaar*, *Women's Wear Daily*, and *Vogue* magazines as the earlier A-line dress gradually loosened up even more from the tighter, waist-emphasizing, form-fitting silhouettes of the fifties and as hemlines kept moving up from their previous midcalf lengths, the fashionable norm of the post-War decade.

A search through the sewing catalogs of 1959 shows that the A-line dress was already merchandised as a pattern shape by Simplicity, Butterick, *McCall's*, and *Vogue* sewing patterns.

The first dress the seamstress made looked like an upside-down cone. It was barely shaped, unadorned, sleeveless, and collarless, with a dart seam for the bosom and a zipper in the back that could be left half unzipped when the weather got too hot. Lilly found that the dress really worked for her daily tasks, so she went back to Woolworth's for more inexpensive cotton fabric and asked the Swiss seamstress to make twelve more similar dresses for her. This time, however, she wanted the dresses to have side slits to allow for even more movement. She thought that some of the slits could be outlined Mandarin-style by white piqué bands and matched by similar white trim around the armholes and neckline. Maybe a few of the slits and the top of a few zippers could be marked by perky little bows.

When the dozen dresses intended for Lilly to wear during work hours arrived, she was surprised by how cheery and decorative they looked, so she put them up on hangers on a pipe rack next to the juice bar. With her suntan, cascading black hair, and big hoop earrings, Lilly looked terrific in these flamboyantly colored and alluringly slit-up shifts. They were lined in fine cotton and required virtually no undergarments, which she claims she always hated wearing. In her bare feet, with her golden eyes and insouciant way of moving about, she looked as if she had stepped out of one of Paul Gauguin's South Seas paintings.

People who stopped to buy orange juice complimented her on the dress she was wearing, and when they noticed the other eleven garments she had hung nearby, they soon scooped up almost every dress from the rack. Then they literally wanted to buy the dress off her back. Lilly can't remember what she charged during these unexpected transactions, but she is pretty sure the price was under twenty-five dollars for each dress. After this first sale, she had twenty more of the pink-and-green or blue-and-yellow floral dresses made, this time with the explicit purpose of selling them. "They took off like zingo," Lilly recalled to *People* magazine.

In countless articles that appeared about the start of her business Lilly expressed her initial surprise at how almost everyone who came to Palm Beach and saw her dresses wanted to take one home with them. She was convinced this was because her dress design represented sheer comfort. Not only in the tropics but even up north, women were ready for them. They were glad to shed skirts and shorts and clothes that bind.

The young woman who was famously known among her friends for not caring anything about clothes and who claimed she had no business sense jumped right in and decided to start a fashion line. But to turn her whimsical enterprise into a real business took skills, ingenuity, and a discipline she had yet to acquire.

CHAPTER 4

Rich, Richer, Richest

WHEN LILLY MCKIM WAS SIX YEARS OLD, HER parents, Robert and Lillian, got divorced.

Robert and Lillian McKim had been a stylish and popular couple, with three lovely daughters. Lilly McKim was the second of the three: blond Memsie (Marie Maude) was considered the beauty; Lilly (Lillian Lee), a brunette, delighted everyone with her originality and mischievous spirit; and redheaded Flossie (Florence) was admired for her poise and congeniality.

Lilly was born on November 10, 1931, and spent her early years in Roslyn, New York, a Long Island community of English-style mansions surrounded by lush greenery: carefully landscaped garden paths and flowerbeds bursting with blossoming hues that appeared as artfully random as the brushstrokes in a Gustav Klimt painting. Fresh vegetables were also grown there for the family's consumption. Life was relaxed, surrounded by beauty and comfort, cushioned at

every turn by servants. During the summer, much of the socializing took place outdoors: pony rides, picnic baskets packed with egg salad sandwiches and ripe tomatoes, elaborate Fourth of July and birthday celebrations, luncheons under striped awnings, al fresco teas, and for the grown-ups, cocktail parties and dancing on the terrace.

All three girls were close to their handsome, witty father. Robert McKim was a successful businessman whose Scottish ancestors traced their assured stance to the early days of the American Revolution. To make amends for a father and a grandfather having sided with the British in that struggle, two sons of the family's original settler, James McKim, enlisted in the newly established U.S. Marines to fight in the War of 1812 against the British. Both were highly esteemed soldiers and are buried in the Congressional Cemetery in Washington, D.C.

One of these ancestral McKims gave his life to save a roomful of comrades by stepping in front of a fellow enlisted man who had suddenly gone berserk and wielded a lancet; consequently, a statue of this McKim was erected in his Massachusetts hometown. The other McKim served as a drummer boy at President George Washington's funeral. Later generations of McKims were lawyers, clergymen, civil engineers, cigar-factory owners, writers of fiction and poetry, abolitionists involved with John Brown, and "lovers of the sea," as the family called them. One of them rounded the Cape of Good Hope seven times in the nineteenth century.

Robert McKim was a cousin of Charles Follen McKim, a founder of New York's renowned belle epoque architectural firm McKim, Mead, and White. They designed many East Coast landmarks, such as the Newport Casino, the Century Association in midtown Manhattan, the Metropolitan Club on Fifth Avenue, and the Washington Square Arch in Greenwich Village.

In one of the most sensational murder cases in New York history, Charles Follen McKim's partner Stanford White was shot

in the head while sitting next to his son in the audience of the original Madison Square Garden, which his firm had designed. The murderer was Harry Thaw, the aggrieved railroad-millionaire husband of White's former mistress, the legendary beauty Evelyn Nesbitt, who was known as the Girl in the Red Velvet Swing. (The story was made into a movie in the 1950s with a young Joan Collins playing Evelyn.)

The McKims were rich, but Lilly's mother, Lillian Stokes Bostwick, a celebrated heiress who had the highest of high-society upbringing, was even richer. Lillian was the grand-daughter of Jabez A. Bostwick, who rose to prominence in New York after making a fortune in the cotton brokerage business in Cincinnati and then turning to the production side of the oil business. Joining the Rockefeller brothers, John and William, and Henry Flagler, the original developer of Florida, Jabez Bostwick became a founding partner of the Standard Oil Company. He served as secretary-treasurer of the Standard Oil Trust, was a major shareholder and the president of the New York and New England Railroad and the Housatonic Railroad, and sat on the boards of the New York Cotton Exchange and the American Cotton Docks. Despite his colossal wealth, Bostwick was known as a modest man of exemplary character and a devout Baptist.

Bostwick died under remarkable circumstances on a balmy Tuesday evening at his summer residence, Friedheim, in Mamaroneck in New York's Westchester County, situated on what is known as De Landey Point, one of the most beautiful spots on the Long Island Sound. When a freak fire broke out at the nearby barn shortly after he had gone to bed after giving a dinner party for friends, he hurried from his house to the stable the moment he was informed of the blaze. He jumped right in with all the men, laboring under great excitement, believing that he ought to personally take part in extinguishing the flames to save the horses and carriages. It took a long time and much effort to bring the fire under control.

Some witnesses swore they saw a falling beam hit Bostwick from the back. Others remembered that after giving a few orders to the men at the top of his voice, he suddenly pressed his hand against his heart and sank down unconscious. Members of his family carried him back to his house, but just as he was finally placed in a comfortable position, he gave a compulsive gasp and fell back, dead. A physician who arrived a few minutes later pronounced that the oil millionaire and railroad capitalist had died of heart failure produced by the excessive excitement of the evening.

An investigation concluded that he most likely died of internal injuries incurred while trying to save his property. While the men were fighting the fire, the coachman and the footman were discovered to be missing. Bostwick could have realized that they might be sleeping in their apartment on the second floor of the stable. Later, when at last an examination of the ruins was made, the charred bodies of the two brothers, Thomas and Henry Atkinson, were found. Whether Bostwick had tried to save their lives is unknown.

The Bostwick family again made headlines when Jabez's widow, Helen C. Bostwick, died in 1921, leaving practically all of her $29,264,181 to her immediate family. The estate consisted of Standard Oil stock valued at $20 million, one-third of which was divided among the five children of her late son, Albert C. Bostwick, who was Lillian Bostwick's father and Lilly Pulitzer's grandfather.

The rest was split between Helen Bostwick's two daughters, Nellie and Evelyn. Nellie Bostwick Morrell was married to a member of the New York Stock Exchange. Evelyn Bostwick was married three times: first to Captain Albert Carstairs of the Royal Irish Rifles, with whom she had a daughter and lived in London; then to Francis Francis, with whom she had two sons and lived in France; and then to Count Serge Voronoff, the noted French gland specialist and surgeon. When Evelyn died, she left her entire estate to Voronoff. This was fiercely contested by her children from

her previous two marriages, so once again the Bostwick name made the newspapers, this time on two continents.

The coverage in the *New York Times* on November 5, 1921, went into great detail about Helen Bostwick's assets after her death, most of which were housed at the family's mansion at 800 Fifth Avenue, which had a stable around the corner at 3 East 61st Street. These included landscape paintings by Jean-Baptiste-Camille Corot and Constant Troyon and a fabled collection of jewelry that rivaled the collection of precious gems owned by Elizabeth Taylor later on.

Among these was a much-discussed string of 133 pearls with an elaborate diamond clasp, a string of 61 pearls with a dramatic ruby clasp, and a three-string necklace of 287 graduated pearls with 15 large diamonds on its clasp. The pièce de résistance—among many other exquisite brooches, bracelets, and earrings—was a string of 80 diamonds with a giant pear-shaped diamond pendant. The pendant alone was appraised at sixty thousand dollars.

What interested Lillian Bostwick and her four siblings much more than diamonds and pearls were horses and aviation. They all enjoyed formidable success in their chosen fields. Lillian's inherited wealth allowed her to become a passionate and outstanding owner of thoroughbred steeplechase racehorses. She won the coveted Grand National with her horses a remarkable eight times. Lillian owned Neji and Oedipus, two of the most prominent horses of the 1950s, which became American Steeplechase Champions five times and were inducted into the U.S. Racing Hall of Fame. Lillian's oldest brother, Albert Jr., turned into a highly respected thoroughbred racehorse breeder whose horse Mate won the 1931 Preakness Stakes (the second leg of the annual Triple Crown, which kicks off with the Kentucky Derby and ends with the Belmont Stakes).

Lillian's youngest brother, George Herbert, known as Pete, probably had an influence later on Lilly—he skipped college,

remarking, "There is no use sitting in school when one can sit on a horse and go somewhere." He became an International Hall of Fame polo player and a U.S. Hall of Fame steeplechase rider. He began riding at age seven at the famous Aiken Preparatory School in South Carolina, where his aunt, Louise Hitchcock, was known as the mother of U.S. polo. Pete eventually reached an eight-goal rating, which is high (ten is the highest), but he also excelled as a jockey and a trainer. Twice at Belmont Park, he made racing history by riding both a flat-turf winner and a steeplechase winner on the same day. In 1962 he was the first steeplechase trainer whose horses won a million dollars in one year. His horses won the Eclipse Award six times.

Lillian's middle brother, Dunbar, straddled the horse world and the airline industry. He distinguished himself on a national level as a breeder of standardbreds. He founded racetracks, pioneered new gadgets and training techniques for harness racing, and was instrumental in developing the magnetic snap barrier, the predecessor of the moving starting gate used today in harness racing. He was co-captain of the 1932 Yale ice hockey team, he was on the U.S. Olympic team, and during World War II he was deputy chief of staff of the 9th Air Force Division, responsible for D-Day planning. He was a recipient of the Bronze Star and the Belgian Croix de Guerre. Dunbar was later chairman of the Aviation Instrument Manufacturing Corporation and became director of the U.S. Trotting Association.

Dunbar, Pete, and Lillian joined forces to build and operate Bostwick Field in Old Westbury, Long Island, where some of the most glamorous international polo matches of the 1930s were held. At the time, polo matches were available only to members of private clubs, but Pete, Lillian, and Dunbar were committed to allowing open participation in this sport, which captivated the public imagination during the depths of the Great Depression.

Lillian's older sister, Dorothy, a painter and sculptor, was the first American woman to hold a helicopter pilot's license. Meanwhile, Lillian's cousin Betty Carstairs became well known in the 1920s as a powerboat racer as well as for her eccentric lifestyle. She dressed like a man, had her arms tattooed, and loved machines, speed, and adventure. She was dubbed the "fastest woman on water" and drove an ambulance for the Red Cross in France during World War II. She was very generous, financially helping several male race-car drivers and land speed record competitors to attain their goals. Betty was briefly married to a French count but reportedly had affairs with several famous actresses, including Tallulah Bankhead. Eventually, she bought the island of Whale Cay in the Bahamas, where she lavishly hosted guests including Marlene Dietrich and the Duke and Duchess of Windsor. She built a lighthouse, a school, a church, and a cannery on the island, then she bought several more islands: Bird Cay, Cat Cay, Devil's Cay, and a tract of land on Andros.

While the Bostwick clan sustained all of these costly sports and hobbies, it did not hurt that several family members married into some of the richest American families at the time. For example, one wed a descendant of the canny patent lawyer Edward Clark, who owned 50 percent of the cash-generating Singer Sewing Machine Company in an age when every woman in the United States had to have a sewing machine.

At the time of the breakup of Lilly's parents' marriage, it was widely rumored that Lillian—or, more likely, Ogden Phipps—paid Robert McKim a million to let her go. Over the years, others have intimated that McKim's final take for agreeing to the divorce was probably even more than that.

In any case, life for six-year-old Lilly and her sisters, Memsie and Flossie, changed a great deal as a result.

CHAPTER 5

Horse Country

WHEN ASKED BY A *VANITY FAIR* REPORTER WHAT her mother and father were like, Lilly answered, "I don't have a clue." It is not due to a loss of memory; it is because of her innate reserve and WASP upbringing. Like former president George H. W. Bush, she has tended to resist being "put on the couch."

If the divorce of Robert and Lillian caused distress to Lilly and her sisters, and if the subsequent absence of their father from the daily lives of all three girls was painful, Lilly has never let the world know it. Instead, she has fondly shared photographs of the dapper, dark-haired McKim, whose handsome face was dominated by striking dark eyebrows and whom Lilly most resembles. One of her favorite snapshots shows him strolling in the park with his daughters in New York City, his arm linked with Memsie's, one hand on Lilly's shoulder and the other holding on to

Flossie. The sisters, dressed alike in dark princess coats with white fur collars and muffs, are the picture of contentment.

Sometime after Lilly's parents split, McKim moved away from Long Island, spending more and more time in Aiken, South Carolina, where he was originally from, and in upstate New York. Several years later, he remarried. Lilly's nature is to be polite and warm, but she can be quick with evasive one-liners if she wants to steer the conversation away from an unpleasant memory or a topic she doesn't like to talk about. So rather than dwelling on her father's departure from her daily life, she has reminisced nostalgically about her childhood visits with him on holidays. In her illustrated book *Essentially Lilly: A Guide to Colorful Holidays,* she told coauthor Jay Mulvaney that she and her sisters would spend most of the summer on Long Island but would always take a break and go up to Cooperstown to see their father, whom she called "Pappy." When coming up with recipes to be included in this entertaining book, she included one of her favorite hot-weather treats, black raspberry ice cream, which had been served in a sugar cone at the country club in Cooperstown where Robert would traditionally take them on the Fourth of July.

For Memsie, Lilly and Flossie these golden days of summer in upstate New York with Pappy McKim, who had family scattered all around Otsego Lake—the history-soaked countryside featured in James Fenimore Cooper's novels—were full of impressionable experiences with aunts, uncles and cousins. Besides Robert McKim's family, the girls also visited lots of relatives on their mother's side—especially their great-uncle F. Ambrose Clark, who had poured his Singer Sewing Machine fortune into splendid horses. In fact, Uncle Brose, as Lilly and her sisters called him, owned most of Cooperstown and, according to Lilly, "had the most beautiful stable I've ever seen." He also had a legendary collection of Sir Alfred Munnings and George Stubbs sporting paintings. Before his famous falling out with his brother Sterling

Clark, one of the most astute American art collectors of all time, whose brilliantly chosen paintings by French Impressionists, Dutch and Spanish Old Masters, and Americans (among them thirty Renoirs and works by Hals, Goya, and Homer, now housed in the magnificent marble gem of a museum near the campus of Williams College), Ambrose and Sterling had made plans to combine their spectacular collections in a single art museum in Cooperstown.

Referred to with affection as the quintessential equestrian sportsman of his generation, Uncle Brose looked as if he himself had stepped out of an eighteenth- or nineteenth-century British sporting painting. Almost always seen in a tweed English cap, waistcoat, breeches, and tall boots, he bred great horses for steeplechase, polo, show jumping and fox hunting at his five-thousand-acre estate. Today the F. Ambrose Clark Award is the highest honor given by the National Steeplechase Association.

Uncle Brose also owned an 11,456-acre plantation for quail shooting north of Tallahassee, Florida, and a sprawling horsey estate in Aiken, South Carolina. He kept a seasonal residence in Melton Mowbray, England, and a New York City apartment in the Dakota, the mystical Manhattan landmark outside of which the Beatles' John Lennon was murdered in 1980 and which was built by Ambrose's grandfather, Singer's patent attorney Edward Clark.

Lilly's mother used to send her daughters' horses up, and Lilly and her sisters would ride every day through the lovely lakeside landscape between the Catskills and the Adirondack mountains. Uncle Brose would drive the three young girls all over Coopers-town in his coach and four-in-hand—a dazzling sight with its four beautifully matched horses. At the end of each drive, he would always stop at the house of one of his innumerable local friends who, most often, were related to him or to Lilly's father, and everyone would have a glass of pink champagne.

Today, Cooperstown is best known as the home of the Baseball Hall of Fame and the Glimmerglass Festival for world-class opera and classic Broadway musicals, but back in the late 1930s and early 1940s, when the McKim sisters regularly spent time there with their father, it was little more than a small village with a few extra families, especially the Anheuser-Busch family from St. Louis, who would come up for the summer months, and the Goodyears from Youngstown, who had a family compound with a huge boathouse at the head of Otsego Lake.

There, every year, according to Lilly, after "the most wonderful parade from Springfield Center to Hyden Hall . . . totally all-American, with Boy Scouts and banners and flags . . . and community sings, Tommy Goodyear would have a picnic on Fourth of July night, just hot dogs and hamburgers." Thinking back on these rustic, close-to-nature visits, and her father's enjoyment of the occasional summer costume parties, Lilly commented, "It was great fun. We just had everything."

What would Lillian's remarriage, in October 1937 at St. Bartholomew's Church in New York, to the esteemed financier and sportsman mean to the three young McKim sisters?

By the middle of the twentieth century, Ogden Phipps was the central figure in the dynasty built on steel and solidified over the years through investment banking, real estate, and the breeding and racing of horses. At the time of the marriage of Ogden and Lillian, the Phipps family owned twenty-eight miles of Florida coastline between Miami and Palm Beach as well as large tracts along Biscayne Boulevard and much of the city of Palm Beach itself. During the Great Depression, the Phipps family was reported to have made several loans to the city of Miami.

Ogden was the son of the steel magnate's fourth child, Henry Carnegie Phipps, known as Hal or H. C., who, through his marriage to Gladys Livingston Mills, brought not only another colossal American fortune into the Phipps family but also enhanced the Phipps name through the pedigree of one of New York's oldest aristocratic and politically distinguished Hudson Valley families. Gladys was the daughter of one of the newest and richest of the new rich, Ogden Mills of California. His father, Darius Mills, had been among the luckiest Forty-Niners. But even though the Gold Rush wealth of the Mills family was immense, the family's social credentials were nil until Ogden Mills married Ruth, the haughtiest of the Livingston daughters, a cousin of the Roosevelts, the Delanos, the Delafields, and the Van Rensselaers, who was descended from the Livingstons who had shaped the Constitution and signed the Declaration of Independence.

In the late 1800s, when many influential colonial families were eclipsed by the robber barons, and social rivalries and games of exclusivity still mattered, Ruth Livingston Mills had challenged her Newport cousin Caroline Astor's famous list of Society's Four Hundred by declaring that only twenty families qualified as "society proper." Ruth and Ogden Mills were said to be the models for Judy and Gus Trenor in Edith Wharton's classic novel *The House of Mirth.*

Ruth, who had inherited the Hudson Valley estate of Staatsburgh from her father soon after her marriage to Ogden Mills, hired the famous society architect Stanford White to revamp the relatively modest country gentry—style structure of the manor house with lavish new wings and a Grecian facade with pilasters, marble balustrades, and statues. Inside were luxurious French furnishings, oak paneling, lots of gilt, and many house parties with a reputation for luxury and social intrigue.

It was through Gladys Livingston Mills Phipps—the august Mrs. Henry Carnegie Phipps, who owned Bold Ruler, the all-time

greatest sire of superhorses, including 1973 Triple Crown winner Secretariat—that her son Ogden Phipps became such an astute horseman. In a 1965 *Sports Illustrated* article, sportswriter Whitney Tower described Gladys this way: "Although she is extremely shy and not given to imperious gestures, Mrs. Phipps must still be considered the grande dame of American racing." It was from her that Ogden inherited the acclaimed Wheatley Stable, which through three generations of Phippses and fifty years of expert guidance in building up the stock became the country's number one thoroughbred racing empire, whose champions would dominate the sport for decades.

Well into her eighties, Gladys enjoyed her amazing success with horses, which she started with a stable of five, concentrating on mares. She would make a list each year of which broodmares were to be bred with which stallions, and she drove her Bentley to the racing stables at Belmont Park three times a week with a passenger cargo of at least three dogs to lovingly feed sugar to her horses. She would pat their heads and talk to them, using appreciative words. She felt no compulsion to grant interviews, and she didn't exactly roar with laughter whenever she came across cartoons of herself in the *Morning Telegraph* or the *Daily Racing Form*.

Lilly's new stepfather was a superachiever. A graduate of St. Paul's School in New Hampshire and Harvard, during World War II Ogden Phipps was a navy officer, rising to the rank of commander. He also rose in the investment banking business at Smith Barney, and from 1958 to 1978 he was chairman of the Bessemer Trust Company, the private bank founded in 1907 (initially to handle the finances of family members only) by his grandfather, Henry Phipps Jr., with the proceeds from the sale of U.S. Steel.

Brought up in a competitive sporting atmosphere, Ogden excelled at golf, boating, and tennis. In the 1930s and 1940s, he won the U.S. Court Tennis Championship seven times, and in

1949 he won the coveted British amateur tennis title. In 2001, he was inducted into the International Court Tennis Hall of Fame.

However, it was in the horse world that he became preeminent, as the owner of numerous outstanding national champions: Buckpasser, which won twenty-five major victories and finished out of the money only once; Personal Ensign, an electrifying filly that never lost a race and won the Breeders Cup Distaff Award in 1988 with its perfect record; Easy Goer, a homebred chestnut colt that won the second fastest Belmont Stakes in history (Secretariat holds the record) and made the American Hall of Fame in 1989; and, of course, inherited from his mother, Gladys, Bold Ruler, the brilliant speedster, Preakness winner, and Horse of the Year in 1957, whose notable offspring include seven of the ten Kentucky Derby winners of the 1970s.

According to Bull Hancock, the legendary twentieth-century horseman at whose Claiborne Farm in Kentucky Bold Ruler served as stud, commanding thirty-five thousand dollars for every mating, "You can pick the Bold Rulers out on their conformation . . . the musculature . . . an extra muscle beside their tail running down to their hocks. It is a good sign . . . it means strength and speed." When Bold Ruler died, sports headlines proclaimed, THE KING IS DEAD.

Sports Illustrated's Whitney Tower wrote about Ogden: "He's as shy as his mother—a trait often mistaken for aloofness—and unbends only with close racing friends or when golfing." Ogden's frequent golfing pal Grumman test pilot Tom Le Boutillier once said of him, "He claims he's a 10-handicap player but he plays to a four and if you let your guard down for a minute he'll empty your pockets. His croquet style putting is murderous." Other friends knew Ogden to be a top bridge player and a whiz at backgammon.

As the thoroughly engaged but low-profile chairman of the Jockey Club for ten years and a trustee of the New York Racing Association, Ogden was the chief guardian of American racing

rules and horse bloodlines. The Phipps family had horses that could outrun competitors and trainers who would make sure that Phipps horses would win. These million-dollar, thousand-pound animal athletes reached peak performance under trainers such as Sunny Jim Fitzsimmons, Eddie Neloy, Bill Winfrey, and Shug McGaughey—all quoted by sports columnists.

Most of Ogden's racing operations were directed from Barn 20 at Belmont Park, where the famous Phipps colors, black and cherry red, flew high. In 1988, Personal Ensign was undefeated and was named Filly of the Year; Easy Goer won the horse world's highest honor, the Eclipse Award for best two-year-old; McGaughey was named top trainer; and Ogden was both the year's outstanding owner and outstanding breeder. Yet in the magically, addictively unpredictable realm of thoroughbred racing, ownership of two of the nation's most mythic equine champions, about which books have been written and movies have been made, eluded the Phipps family.

The beloved Depression-era horse Seabiscuit was born at the Phippses' Wheatley Stable but was judged to have little potential and was sold for a mere eight thousand dollars. By the sporting flip of a coin to determine who would get the first foal out of the mating of the Phippses' stallion Bold Ruler with Penny Tweedy's mare Somethingroyal, the family lost the chance to become the owner of the greatest racehorse of all time, Secretariat.

Ogden and Lillian Bostwick McKim Phipps had two children together. Lilly's half-brother, Ogden Mills Phipps, known as Dinny, succeeded his father as chairman of the Jockey Club and as head of the Phippses' racing stable. Lilly's half-sister, Cynthia Phipps, was an excellent squash player and horsewoman and a major supporter of the Animal Medical Center in New York.

Fighting lung cancer and under heavy medication, she died at age fifty-eight of burns received when her robe caught fire while she was heating water for tea in her Park Avenue apartment.

After Lillian's remarriage, Lilly and her sisters were drawn into the Phipps clan's multitude of activities around the horse-world calendar. Lilly's North Shore, Long Island, riding pals and numerous friends and relatives by blood or marriage such as Dita Naylor-Leyland, Patricia Corey Montgomerie, and Caroline Hudson Firestone recalled the elaborate and elegant Kentucky Derby parties Phipps family members gave on the first Saturday of every May. These were traditionally held on the family's lovely white porches in Old Westbury, where most of the cousins lived.

There were certain formalities. The women traditionally wore dresses, not pants. Mint juleps were served in ice-frosted shimmering sterling cups along with spiced southern pecans and ham biscuits.

Lilly herself never raced thoroughbreds on tracks, though just about everyone in her immediate family has had horses in the Derby lineup. Lilly, always candid and irreverent, liked to quip to her friends that it was surprising that no one in this family of matchless racing fame had ever won the ultimate prize: the "run for the roses" at Churchill Downs in Louisville, Kentucky. Lilly would point out, however, that over the years the Phippses had several Derby runners—a major competitive feat in itself—going back to Gladys with her fabulous champion, Bold Ruler, Ogden with his Dapper Dan, Dinny with Succession, and, most recently, Cynthia with Saarland.

With all the clan's obsession with polo, steeplechasing, harness racing, and breeding (both thoroughbreds and standardbreds), Memsie, Lilly, and Flossie were never far from horses. When they were little, they were often photographed on ponies. Even in the snow, their Shetland ponies, Pete and Sam—one black and white, the other gray—were enlisted to pull the girls up

the hill on their toboggan so they could take the long exciting ride down. As teenagers, the close-knit threesome, perfectly turned out in their velvet-collared riding pinks, velvet caps, and jodhpurs tucked into their English riding boots, would merrily canter along on their flowing-maned white, gray, and bay stallions. A big part of their childhood was fox hunting with the Meadowbrook Hounds. In *Essentially Lilly*, Lilly recalled that "growing up, fall meant only one thing to me: hunt season. We all loved to hunt, so every weekend we would head for the country on Friday afternoon. Saturday, we would get up at 5:00." Long Island neighbors like the passionately horsey Corey children recall that Memsie looked glamorous with her long blond hair caught in the wind as she rode sidesaddle through the sun-dappled woods at the apex of the colorful autumn foliage season. Meanwhile Lilly and Flossie, trying to keep up with their graceful and perfectionist older sister, looked as if they were hanging on for dear life. A groom would always accompany the sisters, ready to pick them up in case they were thrown. Over countless nippy weekends, the three McKim sisters, according to Lilly, "must have galloped through every field and jumped over every fence and every chicken coop on Long Island."

Lilly's mother seems to have been extraordinarily talented at creating the pleasurably informal life that in the last forty years has been synonymous with the Lilly Pulitzer line of merchandise. An effervescent, fun, strong woman with impeccable taste, Lillian was constantly on the go with her Louis Vuitton luggage bearing the old rose-and-yellow stripes of her own racing silks. As active as she was in competing in jumping, riding in the top East Coast events, encouraging participation in her sport, and following the races in which her own and her husband's horses ran, these time-intensive avocations would soon be matched by her fervent involvement in the performing arts, especially in the years after World War II. She became chairwoman of the Saratoga Performing

Arts Center and served on the board of the Metropolitan Opera Association. She was also a community benefactor, a prime mover in establishing the Visiting Nurse Service of New York.

Lillian Bostwick Phipps kept several widely admired homes. There was the estate in Roslyn, Long Island, where she would direct a staff of five in the kitchen, along with butlers, footmen, a laundress, a chauffeur, a ladies' maid for herself, a "mademoiselle" for the McKim sisters, and a Scottish nanny for the two younger Phipps children, Dinny and Cynthia. The first item of the day, brought to her on her breakfast tray, was a menu planner for lunches, teas, dinners, and children's suppers.

There was the large limestone house at 4 East 79th Street in New York City overlooking Central Park, and the seaside Moorish estate in Palm Beach, Florida. Then, with Ogden's New York State racing responsibilities and his role at the Jockey Club, spending the frenetic month of August near the lovely flower-bedecked hunter-green racetrack with red-and-white-striped awnings in Saratoga was added to the family's annual schedules. Here were held some of the nation's most significant races, such as the Whitney Stakes and the Travers Cup.

Ensconced year after year in their beautiful Victorian summer houses at this old upstate mineral spa resort were some of society's most flamboyant personalities: Cornelius Vanderbilt Whitney and his irrepressible hostess wife, Marylou, in her Scarlett O'Hara ball gowns and matching sets of emeralds and diamonds; the popular and outspoken glamour girl and stellar horsewoman Liz Whitney Tippet and her decorated army colonel husband; and *Sports Illustrated*'s longtime thoroughbred editor, the eloquent and amusing Whitney Tower, who was head of the racing museum and on the board of the casino, site of one of the most dazzling summertime balls in the United States. The Saratoga racing season never failed

to attract reigning fashion figures such as C. Z. Guest and often drew major movie stars like Jane Russell at her Hollywood height. Soon Lillian Bostwick added another fully staffed house to her list of homes in Saratoga Springs.

Lillian and Ogden Phipps are said to have acquired and splendidly put together fifteen homes during their marriage. Lillian's interior design team of Robert Denning and Vincent Fourcade have always credited Lillian—along with Ethel Fugg Clift, whose son was the actor Montgomery Clift—with launching their newly minted decorating firm in the late 1950s, when she hired them for major work on her house on Long Island.

By the 1980s, the name Denning & Fourcade became synonymous with colorful rooms densely outfitted with rare eighteenth- and nineteenth-century antiques, museum-quality art, and sumptuous fabrics. "Outrageous luxury is what our clients want," Fourcade once explained to the *New York Times*. Their lush interpretation of French Victorian décor was embraced by such clients as fashion designers Oscar de la Renta and Diane von Furstenberg, art collector and Metropolitan Museum benefactor Jayne Wrightsman, and Henry Kissinger. Their rooms were photographed by every interior design magazine, especially *House & Garden* and *Architectural Digest*.

Their opulent, daringly mixed, and sometimes over-the-top style also became an emblem of corporate raider tastes in the 1980s. The extravagant Park Avenue apartment they designed for takeover tycoon Henry Kravis and his wife, fashion designer Carolyne Roehm, was particularly astounding. It merited an eight-page display in *Town & Country* magazine and served as the on-screen home of the bond salesman Sherman McCoy, portrayed by Tom Hanks in *The Bonfire of the Vanities*, the 1990 movie based on Tom Wolfe's novel about the excesses of the 1980s.

Lillian exemplified the energy, organizational skills, zest for life, and sense of style that Lilly would later exhibit when starting her own business. With all of the perpetual comings and goings, endless projects, and outpourings of imagination on the part of her mother in which she and her sisters participated, it was little wonder that acclimating herself as a young wife to Florida's slow off-season pace would be hard for Lilly.

"I think my mother had a terrific eye," Lilly often said. "She had a very eclectic taste in furniture and loved mixing up wonderful stuff. I had always been around it, it had always been in me." She unquestionably credits her mother's influence on her own bold approach to design and color. It was a "from-the-cradle exposure to Big-E, that is, eclectic taste," her mother's determinedly "mix-it-all-up" credo that blended stateliness with a lack of pretension—fresh and unexpected elements that surprised with coziness and comfort. In Lilly's mind, the famous modern design dictum that "less is more" isn't true—more is more, something she learned from her mother.

In Lilly's private Palm Beach realm, she would deftly place print next to print, pile pillow on top of pillow in a multitude of colors and patterns, and stick pastel-colored candles into unusual pieces of coral, conch shells, and lacy dried seaweed. She created living spaces that were a tropical visual feast, incorporating botanical prints, ceramic elephants, potted palms, painted Italian furniture, plump chintz-upholstered sofas, beaded lamps, paintings by contemporary artists and friends, white Victorian wicker, and brilliant-hued Asian screens.

Lilly developed her own bold and unorthodox ideas on attractive relaxation as well as her trademark style of tropical exuberance and elegant ease, which has come to be marketed as "essentially Lilly" through her two lifestyle books filled with scrumptious

recipes and well-designed table settings, which incorporate her brightly printed Pulitzer table linens with stylized pastel-hued illustrations of guests and hostesses gaily going about these special festivities in Lilly Pulitzer shifts, tops, pants, hats, and long cotton dresses.

Remembering her mother, Lilly told Lorna Koski in a 1994 interview: "She was one fine lady, quite unique. She had a bit of Margaret Thatcher in her. She was born to rule and did what she wanted to do. She loved music, the opera, and ballet. Her passion was doing things. In fact, when she died, she'd just bought an incredible plantation in South Carolina. She was ill in her last few years. She'd had two strokes and a heart attack, but it didn't stop her. She ruled the world from her wheelchair."

Lillian Bostwick McKim Phipps died on November 27, 1987, at the age of eighty-one, in Summerville, North Carolina. She and Ogden had been separated for some time before her death but had not divorced. According to Ogden's niece Dita Naylor-Leyland, the last straw for Ogden was a house-decorating saga that forced him to walk through an elaborate Denning & Fourcade beaded curtain several times a day; it finally made him say, "Enough." Nevertheless, Ogden and Lillian decided that by the time divorce lawyers finished sorting out their wealth, both of them would long be dead.

Ogden outlived Lillian by fifteen years, during which he mostly lived off the Florida coast in his yacht. The Associated Press wrote that from his yacht, Ogden "went every ten days to see his new crop of two-year-olds." Toward the end of his life, he increasingly loved the breeding aspect of racehorses, watching the foals and the mares gamboling in the grass. "The older he was, the more excited he got about the breeding side," the news release said.

Sports Illustrated's Whitney Tower wrote, "The Phippses, however, seldom run second—to other people's horses or to anything else." In the last few generations, they and their cousins married into

families like Grace, Guest, Martin, Mills, Clark, and Bostwick and, according to Tower, "they have become one of the most active and successful sporting tribes of our time." Years ago, Dita Naylor-Leyland concurs, the Phippses used to hunt big game in Africa, shoot grouse in Scotland, and cast for salmon in Canada. "Now we are all fervent environmentalists." More recently, horses and tennis—especially court tennis—have been the dominant family sports. Dashing, dark, and handsome but not tall, Michael Phipps and his over-six-foot cousin Winston Guest were ten-goal polo players," she comments, and Amy Phipps's other son, Winston's brother Raymond Guest, came riding not far behind at eight goals. Ogden Phipps became so enchanted with the old French game of court tennis (today played mostly at private clubs and Ivy League colleges) and subsequently so good at it that only his cousin Alastair Martin ever matched his eight-time national championship. Ogden's brother-in-law (Lillian's brother) Pete Bostwick, another high-goal polo player, once rode in England's prestigious Grand National Steeplechase. Both of Pete's older sons were star court tennis and racquet players and one of them became the amateur golf champion of France. However, while most Phippses and their in-laws rode to hounds, Tower insisted, "No Phipps has ever been a publicity hound."

Although their fierce competition, show of perseverance, and athletic grace took place in a contained universe, the Bostwicks, Phippses, and Guests were highly photogenic. The media, always hungry for news of celebrity and society, regularly recorded them in appealing outdoor settings. They were pioneers of a classic American style that is easy to copy yet still somewhat tricky to truly replicate.

Emulating the aura of aristocracy at ease and wealth at play has continued to be at the heart of modern sportswear, the most significant fashion breakthrough of the twentieth century. Clothing originally designed for movement and flexibility first pioneered

by privileged sportsmen and sportswomen would in time be joined with the fashion needs of active people the world over in an age in which just about everything, work and play, has been sped up and the winners are those who are the quickest.

Lilly's girlhood immersion in her family's disciplined outdoor activities, its sportive manner of dressing, and the hectic and splendid gaiety of informal multigenerational victory celebrations helped to ignite her visual sensibilities and spark her fashion ideas on elegant ease and offhand chic.

Today the sport of polo, often called the sport of kings and rooted in a once-impenetrable world of wealth, has taken a healthy shot at the mass market: it has given life to several of today's global fashion empires. A recent *Financial Times* article quoted Hugh Devlin on Ralph Lauren: "He took a word that was simple, very easy to remember, worked in every language, and also happened to represent his fantasy! Then he made that meaningful to millions of people." The word was *polo*.

Although Lauren has patented the four-letter word to epitomize a luxurious lifestyle, other luxury brands have aligned themselves with the sport to enhance their products' aspirational status. An example is Cartier, the French jeweler, which sponsors international polo games. There's Gucci with its horse-bit gold bracelets and chains and Hermès with its polo-mallet silk scarves. There's the British brand Hackett, specializing in horse-country casuals such as tattersall fabrics and tweedy riding jackets. There are two new popular Argentinean brands, Etiqueta Negra and La Delfina, with merchandise capitalizing on the elegant leather accessories associated with that country's polo tradition and gaucho heritage. And there's Tommy Hilfiger, popularizing and sometimes outrageously jazzing up these once sedate sports classics and making them available at affordable prices. The typical polo attire of bright polo shirts and chinos has become the classic Western male weekend attire—not too different from

what has happened to the Lilly Pulitzer pink-and-green shift that started out as a Palm Beach status uniform.

Lilly was also influenced by several exemplary and stylish women other than her mother. Henry Jr.'s female descendants tended to marry aristocratic Europeans but were in the public eye because of their charities and civic-minded involvements. The philanthropic causes they supported were mostly medical and issues related to underprivileged children and affordable housing. The Phipps men, nice-looking but mostly of average height, were prone to marrying tall, slender, fine-boned, beautiful women with great fashion flair.

Henry Jr.'s spirited firstborn daughter, Amy, added considerable social prestige to the family when she married the Honorable Captain Frederick E. Guest, a member of British prime minister David Lloyd George's cabinet, grandson of the seventh Duke of Marlborough and a cousin of Winston Churchill. At one time he was treasurer of the household of King George V. Amy, a strong-headed and unpredictable young woman, always had a sense of adventure. She was a backer of Amelia Earhart's historic flight around the world and planned to be on the plane, but her parents forbade her to go. According to Peggie Phipps Boegner, Amy used to annoy her parents and brother Jay, Peggie's father, by persistently declaring, "We may be very rich but we are really nobodies. And we will stay nobodies until we marry into the British aristocracy." Which is precisely what she did. Through her propulsive nature, she had managed to skyrocket the social perception of the Phipps family within the time span of one generation onto a whole new level of patrician American standing.

Amy Phipps Guest was a big spender: she lived in what at the time was considered the most breathtaking penthouse in Manhattan, on top of One Sutton Place South, one of the original "cloud palaces" that went up in 1926 and pioneered a new lifestyle for rich New Yorkers on the banks of the East River. But

she was also generous and cared about world affairs. Her Palm Beach estate, with its white-marble-columned folly of a temple to the Greek goddess Artemis between the pristine swimming pool and the deep blue sea, is where Winston Churchill stayed when he visited after World War II. Amy and her siblings opened her late father's mansion, Bonnie Blink, in Great Neck, to about thirty-five British children during the war and donated it along with nine acres of land to the local school district. Troubled by the conflict she foresaw developing in the Middle East, she traveled to Egypt and Israel in 1956, just before the Suez invasion that year, and succeeded in her requests to have private face-to-face meetings with each country's leader—President Nasser and Prime Minister Ben-Gurion.

Henry Jr.'s other daughter, Helen, a delicate dazzler with an authoritative air, also married an illustrious Briton: Bradley Martin Jr., who was related to the fourth Earl of Craven. The ceremony took place at Beaufort Castle, which Henry Jr. rented for a couple of years, near Drumnadrochit in the Loch Ness region of Scotland, amid the pageantry of colorful kilts and age-old highland customs. The couple had four sons, among them Esmond Bradley Martin, about whom the *New York Times* wrote in 2002, "He had an astonishing mind, alive with dynamism and originality that knew no horizon."

An alumnus of Princeton, Esmond was, among other things, a discerning stamp collector, a well-known orchid cultivator, a collector of fine watches, a tennis player who once beat the champion Pancho Gonzales, a world fly-fishing record holder, and a man who excelled at both high finance and wildcatting in oil and gas. His son, Dr. Esmond Bradley Martin Jr., is an ecologist and a world expert on rhinos who has spent most of his adult life in Kenya. Since the early 1970s he has been a prime crusader against products made from endangered wildlife, particularly rhinoceros horns and ivory.

One of the prettiest young women was born in Lima, Peru, and came into the family through Henry Jr.'s oldest son, John

Shaffer Phipps, known as Jay. After graduating from Andover, Yale, and Harvard Law School, Jay decided to attend a fancy ball in London. When he returned that night to his hotel room, he woke up his brother to say, "I have just seen the girl I'm going to marry." Jay did in fact marry the radiant Margarita "Dita" Grace, an heiress whose uncle was W. R. Grace, the founder of the international shipping company and the mayor of New York when the city received the Statue of Liberty as a gift from France. Dita was one of three sisters famed for their flawless faces and slender wasp-waisted figures. They were sometimes referred to as the Three Graces, and they all waited to marry until their late twenties. When Dita was presented at the court of Queen Victoria in a resplendent gown of cascading tulle, glistening pearl shards, and garlands of roses, her picture appeared in the society pages on both sides of the Atlantic Ocean.

Jay and Dita Phipps lived on the grandest scale. Owning property in both Westbury, Long Island, and Palm Beach, Jay initiated the Phipps family's travels between New York and Florida in a private train, originally with nine cars—three for his polo ponies, three for his luggage, and three for his family members and their servants.

One of Jay's finest achievements was his 175-acre estate, Westbury House, designed by George Crawly in the style of Charles II. After Jay's death in 1959, the house and 88 acres of the glorious and unusual series of gardens were opened to the public. Today Old Westbury Gardens receives more than a hundred thousand visitors a year, and on certain summer evenings it hosts free concerts and dancing under the stars.

Jay's son—the gray-eyed polo star Michael, considered the most handsome of the Phipps men—served in air force intelligence during World War II. At a polo party in Calcutta, he caught the eye of a beautiful Bombay-born, Swiss-educated, stylish English woman named Molly Lane. Charmers both, with upbeat personalities,

lovely manners, and exquisite dressing habits, they were the couple whose company everyone in Palm Beach sought out.

Their daughters, Nonnie, who was married to the conductor Thomas Schippers, and Susie, who later turned her commercial acumen to the cultivation of pecans and peaches, were both pacesetters in New York and Florida. Nonnie often appeared in international magazines. The same was true of their cousin by marriage, Stephanie Guest, Winston Guest's daughter-in-law and the daughter of movie star Joan Bennett and producer Walter Wanger. A svelte brunette, she attracted a lot of publicity when she launched several trendy Manhattan restaurants. She was soon followed by 1982's Debutante of the Year Cornelia Guest, who became the darling of the columnists and paparazzi after her brief romance with Sylvester Stallone.

One member of the dynasty commanded the spotlight for half a century. That was Cornelia's mother, a pale-blond, blue-eyed patrician fashion icon and society monarch. The wife of Winston Guest, she was known as C.Z., and she married her distinguished polo-player husband in Ernest Hemingway's home in Cuba in 1947.

Time magazine put her on the cover in the early 1950s as the classic embodiment of the new upper-class American woman. Sassy society observer Aileen Mehle, whose nationally syndicated "Suzy" column irreverently captured the essence of the fashionable world, once described C.Z. as "a woman who shines brighter than others . . . a beauty razor-sharp and diamond clear . . . a snow princess of the north who does not stop at the mechanics of upholding allure. To see her at a party surrounded by brilliantly maquillaged women is to see a sparkling snowflake, drifting by fresh and composed."

Originally from Boston, where she made her debut as Lucy Cochrane, C.Z. briefy became a showgirl and posed for a nude portrait by Diego Rivera. She later gained recognition as an expert

horsewoman and an inspired gardener. A perennial selection on the best-dressed list, she was admired for her choice of clean-lined, trimly tailored, unadorned silhouettes, many custom-made by New York couturier Mainbocher, whose little black dresses and silk-trimmed sweater dress C.Z. helped to popularize. Wearing very little makeup and almost always lightly tanned, she seldom wore fancy jewelry—only a single strand of pearls. Top photographers like Cecil Beaton, Horst P. Horst, and Slim Aarons were enamored of her understated old-guard style and cool modern sportiness. With her self-assured manner and throaty, well-modulated voice, she convinced them to take her picture in simple white jersey tops and shorts, in prim Peter Pan—collared dresses, with a cashmere sweater flung casually around her shoulder, and often barefoot near the pool with one of her pedi-greed dogs. She became the apotheosis of horsey high-society chic.

While all of this was spinning in the adult sphere around her, Lilly, like most children of high-profile men and women like these, lived a sheltered, quiet, busy, and sometimes blissfully barefoot and adventure-filled life far from flashbulbs and journalists.

CHAPTER 6

Of Preps and Debs

L ILLY, THE AVATAR OF PREPPY STYLE, was once very much a preppy herself. During four of her most formative years, she was steeped in this distinct and life-stamping milieu of controlled and disciplined living. As *The Official Preppy Handbook* states somewhat cynically, it's "that magic age" when boys and girls "are passing from unself-consciousness to self-consciousness."

The words *prep* and *preppy* derive from the adjective *preparatory*, which is applied to private secondary schools or boarding academies whose mission is, theoretically, to prepare their students for college or other institutions of higher learning. Although the word preppy has long been familiar to most people inside Ivy League walls, it was the popular 1970 movie *Love Story* that brought an awareness of its meaning to the general public. The heroine in the movie uses it as a term of endearment, but she does so

slightly mockingly, implying that the young man she loves is a rich, pampered elitist.

Of course, not everyone who attends prep school goes to college. But some of the mastered traditions and codes of behavior tend to stick: manners, mannerisms, pet phrases, dress code, and especially the values of diligence, self-discipline, responsibility, an awareness of the consequences of breaking the rules, a passion for sport, fair play, and intellectual rigor. These qualities tend to thrive inside most former preppies as long as they live.

Lilly's teen years were spent at one of the East Coast's most exclusive private boarding schools for girls. For someone of her ilk, there were several options. One would have been Foxcroft School, in the heart of hunt country in Middleburg, Virginia, where equestrian girls from socially prominent families could board their horses while they themselves slept on unheated sleeping porches with flannel sheets and canvas coverings to keep the snow from seeping in. This was meant to develop character, according to the school's legendary founder and longtime headmistress, Charlotte Haxall Noland.

For many pedigreed American families from the Northeast, who favored St. Paul's School (Concord, New Hampshire) and St. Mark's School (Southborough, Massachusetts) for their sons, Foxcroft was the only acceptable school for their girls. With the horsey heritage of the McKims and the Bostwicks in Aiken (South Carolina) and Cooperstown (New York) and with all of the polo playing, horse breeding, horse racing, and other activities of the Bostwicks and the Phipps, one would have expected Lilly to have attended the school that let you board your horse. But no—she went to the other famous school preferred by New York and Philadelphia high society for its daughters: the one Jackie Kennedy had gone to, Miss Porter's School in Farmington, Connecticut.

Nancy Tuckerman, who roomed with the young Jacqueline Bouvier at Miss Porter's—more often referred to simply as

Farmington—and later became her White House personal sec-
retary, explains in William Kuhn's 2011 book *Reading Jackie* what
made the school tick in the 1940s. This sheds some light on why
Lilly's family may have elected to send their daughters there. In
the 1940s, Tuckerman said, Miss Porter's was "very much a family
school. My mother went there, her sister went there, my sister
went there. Jackie's sister, Lee, went there, and their half-sister,
Janet Auchincloss, went there too." This, of course, was more
than half a century ago, long before the school, like most
New England boarding schools and private college preparatory
schools across the United States, began to reach out and create a
more diverse student body both out of a sincere desire to advance
democratic educational opportunities in a changing nation and
to play down its reputation for exclusivity.

In 1945, when Lilly Lee McKim arrived at Miss Porter's School,
her older sister, Memsie, was already there. Sandy (Alexander)
McLanahan, who was simultaneously attending St. Paul's School,
concurred with Tuckerman: "There were a great many very
memorable sisters at Farmington, all at the same time. This
seemed to be not only well-known but often remarked upon by
us even as adult men over the years as we followed their fates.
These girls were very popular with all the guys at St. Paul's, Exeter,
Andover, St. Mark's, Deerfield, Lawrenceville. You name it."
McLanahan's own first cousins, Caroline, Helen, and Prilly
(Priscilla) Husted, were among them. He went on: "There was
Jackie and Lee Bouvier—later Princess Lee Radziwill. Their cousin
Edith Bouvier Beale—"Little Edie" of the movie *Grey Gardens*—
was also there."

The way McLanahan remembers it, "Lilly was two or three years
younger than Jackie. She was wedged somewhere between the
two Bouvier sisters, and she was close to my three cousins, who all
enjoyed her sense of humor and were very fond of her. Of the Husted
sisters, Helen—everybody called her Nell—was the closest to both

Jackie and Lilly. Named after her mother, Helen McLanahan, my father's sister, Nell was highly intelligent and knockout voluptuous, by far the most popular of them all with the boys.

"Caroline, who was scholarly by nature, I remember once called Jackie 'a contrived person.' However, Nell liked Jackie a lot, and Jackie liked Nell. Nell had a serious secret love affair with Jack Kennedy, details of which she decades later insisted on revealing to her children, not unlike these women who periodically come forth compelled to talk about their secret affair with JFK, the president." McLanahan points out that Jackie was for a while engaged to Nell's brother and McLanahan's cousin John Husted.

"I don't think there was anyone who didn't like Lilly. She was cute as a button," McLanahan recalled." I was rather crazy about her myself. She was very appealing. She had a heart-lifting freshness. Her enthusiasm would permeate the room. She exuded health and vitality. You just knew she was a good-hearted person."

According to McLanahan, when Lilly first came to Farmington —and perhaps even before and after—Lilly was somewhat overshadowed by her own sister, whom he remembers as Lilly's "exact opposite. Marie Maude was a stunning blue-eyed blonde. Slender. Very pretty. But ethereal. At times withdrawn."

Like Jackie, Memsie (Marie Maude) and Lilly had both previously attended the Chapin School in New York City. One of the three top-notch private girls schools in Manhattan, it is tucked into a delightfully tranquil corner of the Upper East Side near Gracie Mansion and the sinuous esplanade above the East River. Though academically first-rate and intensely demanding, Chapin was at one time dubbed Deb City because of the school's unusually high number of students listed in the *Social Register*. The following observation, undoubtedly concocted by one of Chapin's rival schools, described the differences among the three schools: Chapin women marry ambassadors. Brearley women become

ambassadors. Spence women dare to become mistresses of ambassadors.

With today's fiercely competitive academic environment at these outstanding but exorbitantly expensive single-sex New York private schools, it would be inconceivable that a student would be allowed to spend three months of the school year in Florida, as Lilly and her sisters did when the family hopped on the annual private Phipps train to Palm Beach and remained ensconced there from Christmas to Easter.

How was schooling handled among these wealthy sun-bound families who yanked their children out of the rigorous intellectual climate, interrupting the vital continuity of certain courses in their schools' required curricula? More important, wouldn't this harm a student's academic achievement, create gaps in the learning process, or affect scholastic confidence? When asked these questions in an interview, Fernanda Kellogg, a child of Palm Beach and later a Chapin graduate, shrugs. "Who knew who was getting an education down there?" she replies. "I don't think anyone gave it much thought. This particular group was so different from today. I don't remember any rigid schooling going on. All the families down there knew each other. Every-thing was always very multigenerational. The Munns, the Wanamakers, the Leases, the Wetherills, the Kelloggs, all were cousins. Everything was very carefree, very family oriented. Children were always running around everywhere. Nannies were rampant. Nobody seemed to mind. There were kids and dogs on the beach and at parties in each other's houses."

She doesn't ever recall the children being called away to do homework or having to excuse themselves because it was time for a math or an English lesson. But surely there were some trade-offs.

Peggie Phipps Boegner reminisced in *Halcyon Days*, her memories of three generations living at Westbury House and

Old Westbury Gardens: "When I was eleven, I went to school at Miss Chapin's, then on Fifty-Seventh Street in New York. This was a strict and fashionable school. I don't remember what I learned there, but I'm sure it gave me a good grounding for future education. Still, I never can see why one wastes time learning Latin and mathematics when there are such interesting subjects as history, literature, and living languages. It was fortunate that although my division was the lowest and the dumbest one in the class, in it were the nicest and most attractive girls. On several occasions, Mother complained to the headmistress that I was too bright to be in the dumb division. Miss Chapin answered dryly that 'it was hard to evaluate Margaret's mental capacity' since I spent most of the winter in Palm Beach."

Apparently, in those days Miss Chapin's School and other private schools were set up in such a way that they would accommodate these children of privilege whose parents traveled back and forth between seasonal homes—and this was when travel was much slower and more cumbersome. This was long before the private Gulfstream or Learjet came to be used by many of today's corporate titans to whisk their families to Bermuda for a weekend or to Aspen, Colorado, for the week from Christmas to New Year's. Back then, children could register for only the fall and spring sessions and skip the winter one, for there were other students who would fill their places during the winter months.

In the book *Sister*, written by her daughter and her granddaughter, Sister Parish, whom Jackie Kennedy later hired to help redecorate the White House, confesses, "If I have very few memories of my first schools, it is because I allowed so few thoughts to enter my head there. In New Jersey, I went to Peck School in the spring and autumn. During the winter, I went to Miss Chapin's School in New York. Somehow, I managed to make it through until it was time for Foxcroft." Her

granddaughter adds, "Once there and for the rest of our lives, the young women became labeled 'Foxcroft girls.'"

But Farmington was not Foxcroft. And Sarah Porter, the founder of Miss Porter's School in 1843, was quite different from Charlotte Haxall Noland, the founder of Foxcroft. Porter was born into an illustrious and learned Connecticut family. Her father, Noah Porter, was the minister of the First Church of Christ, Congregational, 1652, in Farmington for sixty years, and one of her brothers, Noah Jr., was the president of Yale University. Porter received the most advanced education available to a young woman of her era, including tutoring by several stellar Yale professors. A lifelong scholar, she not only mastered four languages in her youth but also taught herself Hebrew at age eighty.

Miss Porter's School started with about two dozen young women between the ages of fourteen and eighteen and today has a student body of 327, of which 210 are boarders. The girls are housed in a dozen handsome historic New England–style buildings scattered on a fifty-five-acre campus on either side of a two-lane highway running through the township of Farmington, a suburb of Hartford. These days, Porter's solemn, chiseled-featured face can be seen in the portraits that hang prominently throughout the school: in the library, in the dining room, and in the office of the school's head.

By the 1940s, Farmington would become known more as a finishing school, "a term you might associate with Mummy's pearls and knowing how to set the table," wrote Evgenia Peretz in *Vanity Fair*. The school was now attended by a generation of debutantes and heiresses, including "poor little rich girl" Gloria Vanderbilt; much-married Woolworth millionairess Barbara Hutton, the most famous American socialite of the 1930s and

1940s; and Brenda Frazier, a beautiful "debutante of the year" who ended up as a recluse. The school's roots were "puritanical and morally rigorous," Peretz noted.

Although Miss Porter's goal was to make her charges good Christians and good wives and mothers, emphasizing the traditional values with which she was raised, the importance of women receiving educations equal to those available to men was foremost in her mind. She hoped that a few of her girls in those first years—mostly the daughters of educators and religious leaders—might become missionaries, but Porter was basically a traditionalist. She believed that the school's atmosphere should resemble that of the home, but, above all, she wanted her pupils to be prepared to pass along to their children the values she held dear.

She firmly believed in the importance of learning Latin, French, German, spelling, reading, arithmetic, trigonometry, history, geography, and service to others. In the nineteenth-century United States, she was convinced that young women were as capable of learning as young men. Her curriculum soon included chemistry, physiology, botany, geology, and astronomy. She also emphasized the arts and hired prominent men to teach drawing and give music lessons. The school frequently gave chamber music concerts, inviting parents and citizens from neighboring Connecticut towns. Each student was expected to design a course selection that would meet her individual needs and tap into her unique talents.

Porter was a firm proponent of the benefits of physical exercise. She banned the long trains on dresses that were fashionable in the late 1800s and asked students to discard the bustles because they limited a woman's freedom of movement. She prescribed daily two-hour walks and encouraged horseback riding and tennis. In 1867, the school formed a baseball team called the Tunxises.

Today, sports remain a vital aspect of the school's identity, with avid interscholastic competition for New England championships

in soccer, volleyball, field hockey, equestrian events, cross-country running, badminton, basketball, squash, skiing, swimming, tennis, golf, track, softball, ultimate frisbee, and that quintessentially prep sport: crew. The tremendous emphasis on excelling at a well-rounded variety of sports and the encouragement of healthy competitiveness are to this day part of the school's template for future lifestyle skills.

These sports competitions echo the grown-up country club experience of politeness and strict rules to be observed, but they are also deeply rooted in the classic Latin creed *mens sana in corpore sano* ("a healthy mind in a healthy body"). It was Porter's profound conviction that the Greek ideal of the fulfilled life consists of a combination of work, play, and educational leisure, achieved through the Socratic model of a concurrence of art, music, literature, debate, and sport.

According to *Miss Porter's School: A History* by Barbara Donahue and Nancy Davis, the girls enrolled in Porter's school in the 1800s were encouraged to perfect such womanly accomplishments as embroidery and needlework while she read to them. As they were working with their fingers, they were exposed to classical literature, history, and the fine arts on the pretext that it would make them more interesting people as well as more pleasing to their husbands and the company they kept.

In the process, Porter activated the minds of some extraordinary intellectual women—most powerfully, perhaps, Edith Hamilton, a graduate of 1886, and her sister, Alice Hamilton, class of 1888. Alice became the first female faculty member of Harvard University and later founded the field of industrial medicine. Edith Hamilton wrote the classic *The Greek Way*, on the calm lucidity of the great thinkers of ancient Athens, a book that Jacqueline Kennedy turned to for solace and answers after the shattering 1963 assassination of the president. A third Hamilton sister, Agnes, was also at Miss Porter's at the time. Another illustrious graduate and a close

friend of the Hamilton sisters was Theodate Pope, who became one of the nation's first successful female architects.

News of Porter's remarkable school spread fast. While she was still dreaming of educating future missionaries, the more fancily dressed, money-flaunting daughters of some of the nouveau riche Gilded Age barons of industry started pouring in. When Porter died in 1900, the management of the school passed to her nephew, Robert Porter Keep, and his wife. After that, their son, Robert Porter Keep Jr., became headmaster. By the 1920s, young women with last names like Rockefeller, Vanderbilt, Havemeyer, Biddle, Van Rensselaer, Forbes, Armour, Swift, Kellogg, and Pillsbury were flooding the place. Although Farmington was never an ordinary school, its reputation as a finishing school was unmatched from the 1920s to the 1950s.

"Women's colleges were now available," wrote Peretz in the *Vanity Fair* article, "but Farmington, according to Farmington, was all that a girl needed. Once the school had given her a good education in the liberal arts, smoothed out her rough edges, and made her shine, she was 'finished' and ready for the proper husband."

Robert Keep Jr. and his wife, RoseAnne, who headed the school from 1917 to 1943, established some strict rules and rituals. At the crack of dawn, the maids would enter the dorm rooms and pull up the shades with a cheerful "good morning." The girls were expected to dress behind screens for the sake of modesty, arrive at breakfast before seven o'clock, and be ready for morning prayers at the Congo, as the school's serenely sleek and lovely old Congregational church was known.

Card playing, gum chewing, smoking, and drinking were forbidden. Touching one's hair during meals was deemed improper, and leaving the school grounds without special permission was not allowed. Unless there was an emergency, there were to be no incoming or outgoing phone calls. Although the students were cloistered from the outside world, many of them flourished in this

atmosphere. Future *Harper's Bazaar* and *Vogue* fashion editor Polly Allen Mellen, the youngest of four sisters, attended Miss Porter's between 1938 and 1942 and had often been heard to exclaim, "I just loved it. Absolutely loved it."

Unlike most similar boarding schools, there was no required uniform devised yet in Mellen's time at Farmington, but the girls there conformed to a look. They tended to wear Brooks Brothers camel's hair polo coats and black-and-white or brown-and-white saddle shoes. Brooks Brothers shetland sweaters, available in a variety of colors, were favorites, worn over neat white blouses and gray flannel skirts.

Mellen through the example of three older sisters and her innate talent for sifting through what was suitable and good-looking in the latest fashions already had a fine-tuned instinct that made her such a first-class contributor to fashion magazines later as an adult. Wearing the right things within the parameters of the school's dos and don'ts came naturally to her, but for less self-confident girls, it was easy to get frazzled and get the dress rules all wrong.

One girl who couldn't quite get it right, despite (or perhaps because of) her twenty-six-million-dollar Woolworth's inheritance, was Barbara Hutton. Some girls worried that their sweaters, blouses, and skirts came from a lesser-status emporium than one of the luxurious departments of a Fifth Avenue or Madison Avenue store, but Hutton—who would later boast among her many husbands movie star Cary Grant, notorious playboy Porfirio Rubirosa, a Russian prince named Igor Troubetskoy, and a Danish count named Kurt von Haugwitz-Reventlow—invoked the disdain of her classmates when she tried to show off with her Chanel skirts and lynx-collared angora sweaters.

There was to be no deviation from the dress code. Still, classmates recall that Mellen managed to reveal her pacesetting individuality by wearing her cardigan sweater backward. Others

tried to express personal creativity through the subtle and minimal signature jewelry that was permitted, such as circle pins, watches, bracelets, and tiny earrings. Nor was there much individuality exhibited among the girls in those years through fancy or imaginative hairdos. Almost everyone wore her hair in a neat chin-length bob or shoulder-grazing pageboy style, recalls another Farmington student of the 1940s.

Lilly, with her dark braids, clearly wanted to make a statement to be different.

The outdoorsy Lilly, who had loved plunging into the big waves at nearby Jones Beach during her Roslyn, Long Island, childhood and was used to rising before dawn to ride with the Meadowbrook Hounds, enjoyed the regimented school days at Farmington. She loved going from class to class on nippy New England mornings when icicles hung from the historic white porticos of the red brick buildings and handsome white clapboard dormitories with dark-green shutters. She relished the fresh snow crunching under her feet as she crossed the picturesque campus. She was less happy when the temperature in September or May would shoot up to ninety degrees, for the girls were not allowed to unbutton their collars, roll up their sleeves, or shed their wool socks and saddle shoes for sandals, much less today's ubiquitous flip-flops.

Even worse than having to tolerate physical discomfort, Farmington students were expected to endure emotional distress, of which there is bound to be plenty at most boarding schools, especially at all-girls' prep schools or colleges. Lilly was fortunate to have her sister Memsie there for comfort, especially in the beginning, which is when most fourteen-year-olds first experience homesickness and loneliness. Later, Lilly's sister Flossie would also come to Farmington, and Lilly was always there for her.

In her *Vanity Fair* article, Peretz, whose mother graduated from Farmington in 1956, related one student's overwhelming initial homesickness, which caused her to cry herself to sleep every night. Her housemother saw that she needed help and brought her into the office of the headmaster. "You are the daughter of a general, now just snap to," the headmaster told her. The schoolgirl recalled, "And I remember standing bolt upright, thinking that I've got to do what he said and behave like I was in the army."

Farmington girls were expected to tough it out and were frequently verbally reminded of this assumption. Learning to accept things without complaint was part of the preparation they were receiving in this system that was training them to be ready not only for the challenges of college but also for the travails they would encounter in the world outside.

There was an unwritten code that self-pity was taboo. "Buck up" was a favorite expression. Surely this would explain Lilly's unwillingness to talk about the negative aspects of her life later, not only with reporters but even with close friends.

Indeed, her schoolmates and boyfriends remember her as ostensibly happy during her Farmington years. As a child, "I was a namby-pamby; people were always making decisions for me," she told *People* magazine's Linda Marx.

But by her second year at Farmington, "Lilly was a leader," according to close boarding school friend Edwina Shea, now Mrs. John Millington. "She was part of the hierarchy of the school." Lilly's most trusted and best friend since childhood has been Kitty Douglas, who, like Lilly, loved horses and riding, but was at another school, Garrison Forest. Kitty would become the wife of Nicholas F. Brady, who later served as a cabinet member of two U.S. presidents. Lilly, as recalled and contemplated by another former Farmington classmate, who grew up partly in New York and partly in Europe, "relied on true-blue friendship and her dry, sharp sting-and-zing wit to balance

struggles she might have had with classwork and dealing with the usual small traumas, romantic hopes, and vulnerabilities we all experienced."

That is how she faced the mysteries, awakenings, and questions of self-worth that characterize the teenage experience. Away from home, Lilly grew freer about asserting herself. She was not exactly impatient to grow up, but she was eager to become her own person.

To this day, Miss Porter's School embodies an atmosphere of educating polished, self-assured girls who look you in the eye, who are remarkably comfortable with adults, and who, in author Kuhn's words, "will one day have a chance both to earn and inherit everything that life has to offer." He maintained that Jacqueline Bouvier was the ideal girl for Miss Porter's, except for one thing: "At the end of the day, when the girls would gather in one another's dorm rooms before lights-out to talk and gossip about the day, Jackie preferred to stay alone in her room reading a book."

He quoted Nancy Tuckerman describing Jackie's reading as "often French *literature*"; she distinctly pronounced the last word the French way to convey the idea of what a proper and academically ambitious school it was when Jackie and she were there together. Tuckerman remembered one girl's mother not wanting her daughter rooming with Jackie "because she thought one point of Miss Porter's was to socialize and meet people," and Jackie was reserved and bookish—not unpopular, but one who liked to spend time in her room by herself.

In temperament, Lilly was just the opposite. She liked mixing with the other girls, making new friends, laughing at all the rituals, and getting a kick out of hearing that someone had gotten away with breaking one of the many rules.

All her life, Lilly has had a coterie of loyal friends who would walk through fire to save her. Her touching combination of bravado and trepidation has always endeared her to her female friends.

The school took it as a prerogative to bring a student's personal shortcomings to her attention. This could be very painful. Girls who were underweight and dangerously skinny were asked to sit together at dinnertime and pretty much expected to eat what was put on the table. Much more embarrassing was the table for "plumpies and dumpies," who were also constantly urged to use the various weight-reducing machines in the fitness department.

Polly Mellen credits her boarding school experience for helping her transform herself from a poor student and somewhat of a plumpie to a svelte and knowledgeable career woman who wielded considerable influence on what American women would wear through fashion magazines, which were not too different from Miss Porter's School in their female hierarchies and the keen competition among editors for pages to accommodate their favorite stories.

Letitia Baldrige, Jacqueline Kennedy's original personal secretary in the White House, a strong-willed and ebullient woman who later worked as a special consultant for Tiffany's and wrote several successful books, was the first student ever on a scholarship at Miss Porter's in the early 1940s. Raised in Omaha, she recalls that her teachers were determined to beat her midwestern twang and Nebraska ways out of her. She remembers that girls with southern accents had to bear similar fates.

Long before Lindsay Lohan mean-girl movies and vitriolic e-mail, boarding school officials were convinced that some of the cruel intimidating tactics of girls in the years immediately after puberty could best be controlled by institutionalizing these impulses. That is how hazing, a rite of passage in most prep schools, came to be. At Miss Porter's School, it consisted of a series of old girl–new girl traditions enforced by a group of "upholders of the rules" who named themselves after Ivan the

Terrible's secret police, the Oprichniki. One can only surmise that some of these humiliating—though also bonding—rituals did not ideally suit Lilly Lee McKim's well-meaning disposition and nice, easy ways.

Jackie Bouvier had a good academic record, which meant that near graduation she was not required to go to study hall but could retreat to her room to read and do her homework. Lilly's friendly nature and outgoing graciousness would have kept loneliness at bay, but her unremarkable academics may have caused her worries. For Farmington was clearly a performance-driven place, both then and now. With each new year, the school became more exacting about a scrupulously increased educational diet of technology and the sciences.

In retrospect, most graduates end up with the attitude "I hate to think of who I would have become if I hadn't gone there." One woman's sentiments express the feelings of many women about how they benefited. She had entered the school with a poor self-image, believing she was stupid, lazy, and trouble. But she was quickly made to feel otherwise. By the end of her first year, she went home having lost weight, free of skin problems, and with As in most of her subjects.

Lilly has also invariably spoken favorably of her prep-school days. And there is no question that her exposure to prep school has imprinted both her and her products' aesthetics. When she was asked by Larissa MacFarquhar in the *New Yorker* to define the frequently used adjective "so Lilly," Lilly answered, "Someone who looks Shiny, Scrubbed, Smiling, Cute, Comfortable, Care-free, Without Worries, Graceful at Leisure." It could be a description of the perfect preppy.

By the 1940s, private schools lived on the achievements of their impressive marketable products, the distinguishing marks made by their notable alumnae. The roster of famous Farmington girls is staggering: among them, besides Jacqueline Bouvier Kennedy,

Lilly McKim Pulitzer, Polly Allen Mellen, Gloria Vanderbilt, and Barbara Hutton, are Academy Award–nominated actress Gene Tierney; food legend Julia Child; ambassador Anne Cox Chambers; movie star and social activist Dina Merrill; Emmy Award–winning actress Barbara Babcock; budding Broadway actress Mamie Gummer (Meryl Streep's daughter); authors Letitia Baldrige and Pema Chödrön (formerly Deidre Bloomfield-Brown and now a Buddhist nun); novelist Ruth Pine Furniss; former president George H. W. Bush's mother, Dorothy Walker Bush, and his daughter, Dorothy Bush Koch; philanthropist and socialite Laura Rockefeller Chasin; and Elizabeth Cushman Titus Putnam, founding president of the Student Conservation Association (SCA) and recipient of the Presidential Citizen's Medal.

The motto of Miss Porter's School is the Latin *Puelae venerunt. Abierunt mulieres* (They came as girls. They left as women.). The school has figured in about a dozen novels, movies, and television series, from *Buffy the Vampire Slayer* and *Dynasty* to Katharine Hepburn's 1938 movie *Holiday* and Whit Stillman's *Metropolitan*, the poignant 1986 film about New York debutantes.

In the 1940s and 1950s, a young woman like Lilly with an American blue-blooded lineage was expected to make a formal bow into society. In interviews during the rebellious late 1960s and early 1970s, when the zeitgeist frowned upon such old-guard frivolities but which coincided with the peak of media interest in Lilly as a successful designer, Lilly played down the notion that she had had a debutante party. In fact, she had had two of them: one on Long Island and one in Palm Beach, according to her friend Sandy McLanahan.

On January 4, 1950, the *New York Times* mentioned Lilly as one of the debutantes being feted at the Black and White Ball along with her Phipps cousin Dita Douglas and fledgling socialites

Evelyn Rogers, Evelyn Harris, Marilyn Milton, and Louise Wheeler. In a February 1, 1950, *New York Times* article, Lilly is listed among "a group of debutantes of this season serving on the Social Committee," assisting at a luncheon benefit for the Downtown Beekman Hospital.

Lilly followed in the footsteps of her sister Memsie, who made her bow to society at New York City's most prestigious debutante ball at the time, the Infirmary Cotillion. Memsie was cochairwoman of the debutante committee at the December 22, 1947, Christmas Ball, which honored 130 young women from some of the city's most old-line families—the Winthrops, the Paysons, and the Aldriches—as well as Memsie's good friend Beverly Brady, sister of a future secretary of the treasury, Nicholas Brady.

Lilly insisted that she did not like cotillions very much. When asked by *Vanity Fair*'s Laura Jacobs whether she had a coming-out party she replied, "I had a party every year, and one of those, I guess, was my coming out." She most warmly remembers her younger sister Flossie's debut, which was a costume party at which Ogden and Lillian were dressed as Farmer and Mrs. McGregor and the three girls were the rabbits Mopsy, Flopsy, and Cottontail. Actually, they were not cute little cottontails at all; appearing in fishnet stockings, shiny white satin shorts, ruffled blouses, and amusing floppy-eared headdresses, they looked more like Playboy bunnies.

There are indications that Lilly was less inclined to go through the various motions—debutante parties and charity events planned to launch a young socialite in a city like New York—than her two sisters were. But neither did she fight it. She did what was expected of her, given the social standing of her family. In those days, turning seventeen signaled that the time had come for her to be formally introduced to Society with a capital S. The forties

in the United States was an era of great glittering parties, one grander than the next.

The tradition of a debutante making her formal bow had actually begun in Baltimore in the 1600s. By the time Lilly came of age, the custom was deeply ingrained, especially on the East Coast. In Philadelphia, the parties were given at the Barclay Hotel. Proper young Bostonians were expected to be presented, according to social historian Cleveland Amory. In New York City, the parties were most often held in the ballroom of the Ritz or the Pierre. But on Long Island, where the McKim girls made their debuts, colossal striped tents created rooms much larger and more breathtaking than any ballroom.

Party after party, with the young men in white tie and the young women in white satin gowns, most of the same people danced to the same Cole Porter and George Gershwin tunes played by Lester Lanin, Meyer Davis, or both. They went to similar small private dinners beforehand, drank pretty much the same brands of champagne, ended the festivities with scrambled-egg suppers at dawn, and then exchanged the same gossip the next day. Lilly's mother's social secretary would plan each girl's coming-out party for months.

All in all, Lilly's girlhood friends at Miss Porter's School were an exceptional group of young women, poised at an early age to make their mark on the world at large. An uncommon number of her closest chums would later shine in the public light. Even though their families expected them to one day stand firmly and proudly by the side of a prominent man, none of the women settled for being just arm candy.

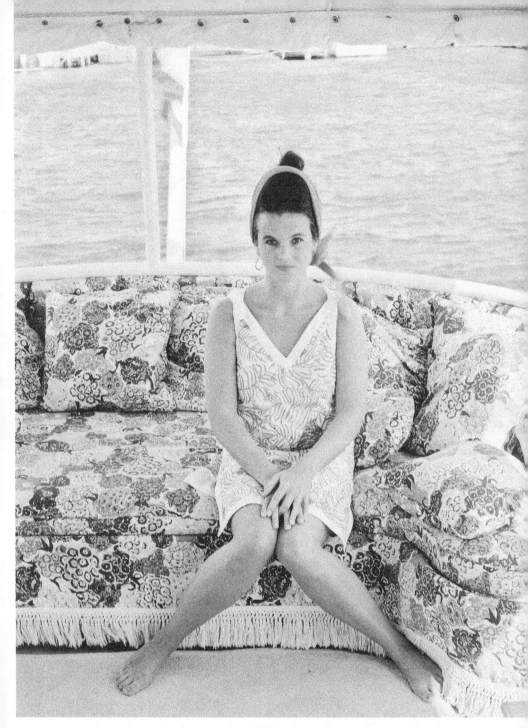

On board the *Vergemer*, the 118-foot yacht belonging to her mother and stepfather, Lilly Pulitzer wears one of her early cotton Lillys.

Lilly McKim on one of her beloved horses during her prep school days.

Lilly in her first boutique on Via Mizner in Palm Beach, just off Worth Avenue.

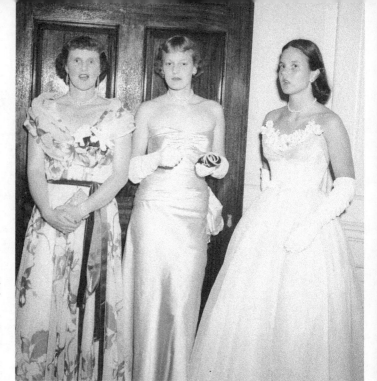

Lilly (at right) with her mother, Lillian Bostwick McKim, and her sister Memsie in the receiving line at Lilly's debutante party in Westbury, Long Island.

Lilly's mother, Lillian, enjoying an elephant ride with her three daughters at the Westbury Fair on Long Island in 1936. From left to right: the eldest, Marie Maude, known as Memsie, Lilly, and Florence, known as Flossie.

Lilly dashes with fabric swatches from Peter's seaplane, which had just flown from the Pulitzer hand-printing operations in Key West to her sewing factory in Miami.

Young Palm Beach matrons and their daughters in their Lillys gathered around a fountain in 1964.

Lilly in her late teens (at far right) with two Long Island chums, her Phipps cousin Dita Douglas (left) and Edwina Shea (middle), about to take in the action at a polo match.

Dining and dancing away the tropical night under the stars at the Patio, a favorite of the fashionable Palm Beach resort crowd in 1940.

First Lady Jackie Kennedy wearing an early red-and-white checked gingham Lilly shift, with the president and her children in Hyannis Port, Massachusetts, in 1962. This photograph helped catapult the Lilly Pulitzer fashion brand to national fame.

Basking in the South Florida sun, Lilly and Peter shortly after their elopement to Maryland.

Lilly and Peter in the early days of their marriage on their way to a Palm Beach black-tie party in the winter of 1954, with friends Patricia Massie Tevander and Alexander Cameron.

C. Z. Guest, whom *Time* magazine put on its cover as the epitome of mid-twentieth-century American high-society chic, at the Palm Beach home of her mother-in-law, Amy Phipps Guest.

Lilly's mother and stepfather, Lillian and Ogden Phipps, at the
opening of her art gallery in Palm Beach, 1965.

Polo enthusiasts in the winner's circle at Long Island's Bostwick Field in 1937. From left to right: Charles Von Stade; Dunbar Bostwick; Laura Curtis Bostwick; Laura's husband, Pete Bostwick; and Laura's brother, James F. Curtis Jr. Bostwick Field was founded and operated by Bostwick siblings Dunbar and Pete and Lilly's mother.

Clark Gable on one of his many visits to Palm Beach during the high season, on Worth Avenue in 1937 with popular local socialite Dolly O'Brien.

C. Z. Guest (standing) with the Duke of Windsor and film star Merle Oberon at the polo ball in Boca Raton in 1956.

Peter and Lilly Pulitzer had three children in the first four years of their marriage. First-born Peter Jr. is protectively holding on to his little sisters, born barely more than a year apart: blond Minnie on the left and dark-haired Liza on the right.

Dashing cousins Michael Phipps (left) and Winston Guest, among the highest-ranked polo players of their day, epitomized the classic American sporty look that inspired Ralph Lauren, Tommy Hilfiger, and other designers worldwide.

The patriarch of the Phipps clan and Andrew Carnegie's partner, Henry Phipps Jr., around 1857.

The Phipps cousins present William Shakespeare's *A Midsummer Night's Dream* in Palm Beach in 1914. Lilly's stepfather, Ogden Phipps, third from the left and wearing wings, played the role of Puck.

Multimillionaire businessman Peter Pulitzer at the height of his manly allure.

Newspaper magnate Joseph Pulitzer at age twenty-three, when he was a reporter in St. Louis.

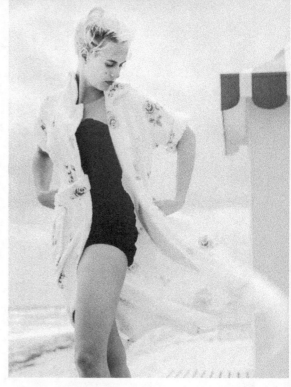

Peter's sister, Patsy Pulitzer, was considered a smashing beauty and for a while modeled professionally, represented by the Ford Agency.

Peter Pulitzer's father, Herbert "Tony" Pulitzer (with eye patch), son of Joseph Pulitzer, entertains his family and international friends at his Lido Beach cabana in Venice. The blond woman on the blanket, far right, is Tony's daughter, Patsy Pulitzer Bartlett.

In the garden of her first house in Palm Beach, Lilly pouring a glass of lemonade for her daughters, Liza (with one of the family's many dogs about to climb into her lap) and Minnie.

Alina Johnson Aguilera (with hat) and her friends personified the stylish young society women of Havana in this 1950 photograph, part of a story that ran in *Life* magazine.

Enrique Rousseau, playing the guitar, with Lilly next to their favorite Palm Beach pianist, Marshall Grant, in an impromptu jam session at Grant's restaurant.

Lilly found lasting love with her second husband, Enrique Rousseau, an American-educated Cuban lawyer from a patrician family, who was protective of her and shared her zest for life.

Harvard MBAs Scott Beaumont (left) and James Bradbeer convinced Lilly to make a comeback, something rarely done in the fickle fashion industry.

With her daughter
Liza Leidy, Lilly
having fun with
Bobby, one of her
grandchildren.

Lilly adjusting
an outfit from the
brightly colored
clothing line
embraced by a
whole new
generation.

CHAPTER 7

Falling in Love with a Pulitzer

AFTER ATTENDING MISS PORTER'S SCHOOL in Farmington and enjoying the debutante parties, one grander than the next, Lilly and her friends were consumed by thoughts of the future and hopes of finding true love. Most young American women of the 1950s, even the most educated or privileged ones like those in Lilly's circle, were basically longing for one thing: to marry the men of their dreams.

Many of her friends eased into student life once more by going to college. Lilly was never much of a student. "She and I were the worst," recalls her childhood friend and classmate Edwina Millington. "We were at the bottom of the class at Farmington. I was dyslexic and she was bored. Instead of studying, she just went off riding her horse."

Friends and family were astonished by Lilly's next moves. After no more than a few months at Finch College, Manhattan's Upper East Side junior college, which began

as a finishing school but later evolved into a four-year bachelor's-degree-granting college with a strong art program, she quit school. Then came the nurse's aide stints in the Kentucky wilderness and at the Veterans Hospital in the Bronx. By early 1952, her friends remember, she seemed rather adrift, unfocused about the future.

One of her good friends and classmates from Miss Porter's School, Nancy Moorland, a tall, lithe blonde who grew up a few apartment houses down Fifth Avenue from where Lilly's family had lived, had already established herself as a well-paid, steadily working fashion model, her beautiful, even-featured face and sparkling blue eyes smiling from advertisements and the occasional cover of a magazine.

Nell Husted, a full-blown dazzler with a tumble of dark curls framing her pale white skin and intense black eyes by the time she was enrolled at Bennington College and majoring in Russian, already had mastered Spanish through lengthy stays in Mexico. She was the steady girlfriend of future independent filmmaker and actor John Cassavetes, when during a visit to Washington, D.C., she met a Russian prince, a graduate of Andover and Yale, named David Chavchavadze. Her tempestuous romance with the prince did not go into full gear until she spent her junior year at the Sorbonne in Paris to perfect yet another language, and Chavchavadze, working for U.S. intelligence, was stationed in Berlin dealing with a series of suspenseful Soviet defections. They married in 1952, after which Nell was able to utilize her fluency in several languages as a translator of top-secret documents.

As of January 1952, Jacqueline Bouvier, who had been a year ahead of Lilly at Farmington, had landed the job of "inquiring photographer" for a lively newspaper, the *Washington Times-Herald*, which was outselling both the *Washington Post* and the *Evening Star*.

Jackie was clever, pretty, and artistic. Her intensely competitive nature and distaste for defeat were apparent even to her most devoted friends during her pursuit of horseback riding and fox hunting. When she graduated from Miss Porter's, her yearbook page stated her ambition "not to be a housewife." She had managed to use a Speed Graphic camera, and although her job was not particularly intellectually demanding, she was able to apply her considerable creativity to it. Her assignment was to ask people on the streets of the nation's capital or in their government offices, after she had snapped a photo of them, about the news of the day.

In typical Jackie fashion, she took serious care each day to prepare provocative, even personal, questions in order to elicit quotable answers. She was determined to have her column reflect favorably on her. She would ask, "Chaucer said that what most women desire is power over men. What do you think women desire most?" or "Do you think a wife should let her husband think he's smarter than she is?" The job provided Jackie with access to the influx of newly influential and exceptional people to Washington in the postwar years, when the city was not only expanding in size but also growing in international importance.

So it was by using her newspaper column that Jacqueline one day called witty, wealthy, good-looking, bachelor war-hero Jack Kennedy, then a senator, whom she had met at a dinner party in 1951. Several members of Kennedy's office staff later remarked that Jackie's column played an important part in rekindling their acquaintance and in letting the popular young politician know that Jackie was more substantial and literary than most of the other former debutantes or attractive young women Jack dated.

Shortly thereafter, Jackie broke her engagement to John Husted, a rising young investment banker, the socially prominent brother of Lilly's other close Farmington friends, Nell, Priscilla, and Carolyn Husted. The senator from Massachusetts was, it seemed, any woman's dream come true.

Many of Lilly's boarding school pals were leaving top Seven Sister colleges without graduating to get ready to be married before Christmas or in June. They would plan elaborate wedding days and festive occasions such as engagement parties and bridal showers. There were thousands of things to accomplish in order to stage these nuptial extravaganzas—for instance, in white wonderlands of Connecticut snow with evergreens and twinkling lights for the driveway, mistletoe hanging over the doorways, and garlands of pine and green leaves festooning the banisters and fireplaces. There was no such thing as too much time spent on engraved invitations, bridesmaids' dresses, and registering in stores to select china and silver from Tiffany's or crystal from Steuben and Baccarat.

Some of Lilly's friends who had opted for work rather than college were giving up prestigious though low-paying editorial assistant jobs at *Vogue* and *Harper's Bazaar* to redecorate apartments or prepare to move to plantations in South Carolina, horse farms in Kentucky, or suburban mansions in wealthy Midwestern enclaves like Lake Forest, Illinois, with Harvard, Princeton, or Yale graduates who would enter the family business and with whom they wanted to start a family right away. One of these young women, originally from New York reflected years later, "There seemed to be such a rush."

In the protective atmosphere of boarding school, with all of the curfews and other rules, it had been easier to be cautious. But in the fast-moving social whirl of places like New York and Palm Beach, they recognized that no matter how attractive or rich a girl was she could be rapidly replaced in the heart and mind of the young man she loved. Competition was keen. It kept you on your toes. And sometimes the men who found you enchanting didn't necessarily want to marry you. In fact, they frequently married

FALLING IN LOVE WITH A PULITZER

more plain, less physically appealing and even homely women who they assumed would make safer, better wives.

In the 1950s, if a young woman was virtuous, she was usually rewarded with a marriage proposal sooner or later. Young men were less averse to commitment than they are in today's free-for-all sexual climate. Although a young woman might try to make her boyfriend jealous in order to coax an engagement ring out of him, if she actually played around, she could be the target of nasty gossip. Sometimes a free spirit paid a heavy price for her flirtations, and a girl who was perceived to be two-timing could land right out of the marriage market. It was drummed into the heads of these young, rich and pretty women that timing was everything. An opportunity that was missed might never come again.

Lilly was energetic, enthusiastic, and playful, and she was very popular. "She was just wonderful, really adorable, very sweet," recalled Sandy McLanahan, a student at St. Paul's School and Yale as well as a first cousin of Jackie Bouvier's former fiancé, John Husted. "She was loads of fun, spontaneous and natural, never snobbish, always respectful and kind to others. Still, she was a little different; with her dark braids and mysterious eyes, she looked like Pocahontas. She was a lot more colorful than many of the other girls who had a similar upbringing."

Her pal Edwina Millington added, "She was funny. Really could make the boys laugh. They loved her language, which could make the wallpaper peel. There was no one like her. Totally uninhibited in what she would say. She was probably the most popular of us all with men in those days, when many of us were still shy or simply didn't know what to say to amuse and entertain the opposite sex."

But according to another of her boarding school confidantes I interviewed, Lilly was also old-fashioned and a romantic. "She dreamed of heart-pounding, gut-numbing, euphoric love. If there

121

was an element of danger to the dashing man of her dreams, all the better. But he had to be handsome and he had to need her as much as she needed him." Lilly's friends agreed that she decidedly had a weakness for " drop-dead handsome men." One New York acquaintance of Lilly's remembered how Lilly once teasingly tried to push her uncommonly good-looking future husband—dashingly dressed for a poolside cocktail party in a brand-new double-breasted navy blazer and perfectly pressed white linen trousers—into the swimming pool near the edge of which he was standing sipping a vodka and tonic. This woman was not yet engaged to the young man but remembered being at that moment very jealous of Lilly's light, humorous touch and daring ways. Then she added, "People like us who knew we were so lucky to have been given so much in life, we were always afraid that when everything in your life was perfect, it would all suddenly vanish."

Quite unexpectedly, on a May afternoon in 1952 when she was supposed to be meeting a friend for tea on Long Island, Lilly ran off to Maryland to marry Herbert "Peter" Pulitzer Jr., the golden-boy grandson of legendary press magnate Joseph Pulitzer, a young man thought by many to be the most exciting catch in Palm Beach. Before meeting Lilly, he had briefly dated the young actress Grace Kelly, then still living in New York City, as well as Jacqueline Bouvier, before she met Jack Kennedy. Lilly was not quite twenty-one.

Few people seemed to be aware that Peter Pulitzer and Lilly McKim even knew each other; therefore, all of their intimate friends and both of their families were in shock when the couple secretly married in a ceremony conducted by a Baltimore justice of the peace. What stunned people even more was that Lilly and Peter announced that they planned to live year-round in

Florida—even through the tropical torpor of the summer months, something no one with their wealth and alternatives did in those days.

Florida, before the Eisenhower project of interstate highway construction, was quite a different place. Much of the area was still underdeveloped and forbidding. Even air-conditioning was far from the norm. Once the glittering resort months were over, most things came to a primitive standstill.

Peter and Lilly had met and their romance had secretly blossomed in Palm Beach. Although it is frequently said that Lilly chose a husband against type, it was actually not that surprising that Lilly and Peter got together and fell passionately in love. In Palm Beach, the big Phipps oceanfront estates and the Pulitzers' property were not that far away from each other: the Pulitzers, on Wells Road, living on a part of what was once the grand estate called El Mirasol, designed by the architect who had set the tone for the resort's Spanish fantasy look,were just to the south of Ogden and Lillian Phipps's unique Moorish house, a palatial replica of the Alhambra, where as described by Lorelle Hearst, a columnist for the Palm Beach *Daily News*, Lillian in her favorite blue satin Moroccan caftan, embroidered with real gold threads, liked to give Orientalist-style dinner dances and entertain the likes of Truman Capote and Gloria Guinness.

Ogden, as his Phipps-born niece Dita Naylor-Leyland remembers it, early on detected romantic sparks flying between his playful, innocent, but ardent and impulsive stepdaughter and Peter Pulitzer. And he did not approve of the possibility of a marriage between the two. Ogden was out-and-out against Lilly ending up with a young man whose parents seemed to have been always traveling in Europe, who along with his sister, in his opinion, had been brought up almost like orphans, left entirely in the care of nannies while their mother and father were away. Ogden perceived Peter as someone who tended to resist authority

figures and who was defiant and fast, most damningly,a playboy. Ogden at the time was the all-powerful and highly consevative head of the Phipps family's financial arm, the Bessemer Trust; therefore, almost the titular head of a family that had been tra-ditionally careful about whom they married. In Dita's words, "He was austere. In fact, he could be terrifying."

According to Lilly, she and Peter were introduced by his sister, Patsy, who like Lilly had attended two of the so-called right private schools: Palm Beach Day School in Florida and Foxcroft School in Middleburg, Virginia. Patsy and Lilly both had been students at Finch College but Patsy did not drop out and earned an associate of arts degree there, something she later utilized as a major supporter of the Society of the Four Arts in Palm Beach. In 1952 she made national news when she caught the world-record fish for a woman, a black marlin weighing 1,230 pounds, off the coast of Cabo Blanco, Peru. The December 25, 1961, issue of *Sports Illustrated* listed her as one of "the World's Loveliest Sportswomen."

Patsy was first married to a very attractive and popular East Coast—educated Chicagoan, David Bartlett, a former U.S. Marines officer who had served in the Pacific during World War II. Bartlett's father was a banker of national prominence, and his family had wintered in Hobe Sound, an even more exclusive social enclave than Palm Beach, on Juniper Island, up Florida's Atlantic coast, In those days Hobe Sound was "restricted," a community whose residents had to be members of the club and had to be WASPs. David Bartlett had a promising career on Wall Street.

David would later be devastated, and tongues were wagging from New York to Palm Beach, when Patsy abruptly left him with their two daughters to marry an even more successful banker, Lewis T. Preston, later president, chairman, and CEO of JP Morgan. In 1990, at a historic moment shortly after the fall

of the Iron Curtain, Preston was named head of the World Bank. When this happened, David's brother Charlie Bartlett, a longtime Washington insider and presidential confidant of both John F. Kennedy and George H. W. Bush, consoled him by saying, "What did you expect? The Pulitzers were brought up in Palm Beach. They have different values."

Peter and Patsy's father, Herbert "Tony" Pulitzer, was a tall, lean, rakishly handsome man who sported an eye patch. At one time the publisher of the *New York World*, he was smooth and cut a glamorous figure in such postwar hot spots as Cannes in France and the Lido in Venice, where he annually rented a cabana along the spiral-striped pillars and awnings of the beach. On his scattered black-and-white checkerboard pillows and sun mats, he entertained a dazzling array of dolce vita Italian princesses and starlets, English duchesses, and expatriate Americans like Peggy Guggenheim.

Tony Pulitzer was the youngest of Joseph Pulitzer's sons. Joseph, an adventurous Jewish young man of vaulting ambition who emigrated at age seventeen from Hungary, became one of the greatest and most powerful U.S. newspaper publishers a few years after he landed in Missouri. He later established the Columbia University School of Journalism and one of the most prestigious awards for news reporters, photojournalists, playwrights, poets, novelists, nonfiction writers, and composers: the Pulitzer Prize.

Although most people are familiar with the Pulitzer Prize, few know much about the man who supplied the name. The teenage Joseph left Hungary alone and lied about his age in order to enter the United States as a paid Union soldier. After the Civil War, he slept on park benches until he found work tending mules, waiting tables, and serving as a coachman while still learning to speak

English. Within five years he had gotten elected to the state legislature in Missouri. Within seven years, he had become the publisher of a local newspaper, and soon after, he founded one of the nation's most highly respected newspapers, the *St. Louis Post-Dispatch*. Then he bought the *New York World*, which in the 1880s became the largest-circulation paper in the country.

Over the years he persuaded some of the most gifted editors to work for him. He lured John Cockerel from the East Coast to St. Louis, where the two men changed the face of American journalism with their innovative style and aggressive reporting. His brilliant newsman Arthur Brisbane, who was highly instrumental in the success of the *New York World*, would in turn be persuaded to leave by Pulitzer's greatest rival, William Randolph Hearst, with whom he was in a crippling circulation war that almost bankrupted both of them and led to the age of sensational "yellow" journalism.

Pulitzer held major political sway for decades and amassed great wealth. Even though he criticized the elite in print, he was one of the fifty richest Americans by 1891, with a huge columned mansion on New York's Upper East Side, a palatial estate on Mount Desert Island in Maine, and another elaborate home for winter escapes on the millionaires' private resort Jekyll Island off the coast of Georgia.

Pulitzer was high-reaching, hotheaded, and sometimes violent; he was shrewd in matters of business and cold in matters of the heart. Despite his success, Pulitzer was a tortured and suspicious man. He spent much of his adult life on his yacht, the *Liberty*, which was the length of a football field and had a forty-five-man crew.

In later years, as he was losing his sight, he became obsessed with his health. He traveled to Europe's top spas, and with a retinue of personal aides, he was in exile from his wife, Kate, and their children. He continued to micromanage his staff

long-distance, setting up talented men in key positions but in a strategic conflict-causing way that would force them to inform him about one another.

Joseph Pulitzer lived in an era, as Hearst did, when newsroom scores were sometimes settled with pistols, anti-Semitism was rampant, out-of-work politicians became newspaper editors, and successful editors became elected politicians.

Joseph, who did not attend synagogue or participate in Jewish life in the United States, married Kate Davis, an Episcopalian and the daughter of landed southern gentry. They had six children: Ralph; Joseph Jr., known as Joe; Herbert, known as Tony; Constance; Edith; and Lucile Irene, her father's favorite, who died young. Joseph's will, read a few days after his burial in late October 1911, surprised his children. He left the *New York World* and the *St. Louis Post-Dispatch* in the hands of four trustees, who would later have to turn control of the papers over to Joseph's three sons.

Pulitzer's estate, excluding his homes in Maine and Jekyll Island, was valued at $18,645,249.09, according to a 2001 biography of him by Denis Brian. What really astonished everyone was how Joseph divided the company stock. Herbert "Tony," the youngest but his father's favorite son, who was fifteen at the time and had done little more than visit one of the newspapers, was given 60 percent of the stock. Ralph, who had been pretty much running the *New York World* during his father's ailments and absences, was given 20 percent; and Joe, the most journalistically talented of the three, who had often infuriated the father with his own news instincts and independent opinions, was penalized for this and received a mere 10 percent. The remaining 10 percent was to be used for producing income for the editors and managers of the papers. Power was

more equally divided among the sons. Each son would eventually have a seat on the board and each member of the board would have one vote.

Kate, Pulitzer's fifty-eight-year-old widow, never remarried. She lived mostly in France—Deauville, Cap Martin, and Nice—after her husband's death but was buried next to him in 1927 at Woodlawn Cemetery in New York City. She was left with a $2.5 million trust and the use of the houses. Pulitzer's daughters—Constance, who married the son of a British judge, William Grey Elmslie, and moved to Winnipeg, Canada, and Edith, whose husband William Scoville Moore was the grandson of the author of *The Night Before Christmas*—would share the income from a $1.5 million trust. To the city of New York, Joseph left the fountain in front of the Plaza Hotel and a two-million-dollar endowment to the journalism school at Columbia University, with its prestigious national prizes. He also left $1 million each to the Metropolitan Museum of Art and the New York Philharmonic with the explicitly stated hope that the orchestra would continue to play his favorite composers, Beethoven, Wagner, and Liszt.

The man who had ushered in the modern mass media in the United States had one clear final instruction for his heirs: "the duty of preserving, perfecting, and perpetuating the *World* newspaper, to the maintenance and publishing of which I have sacrificed my health and strength, in the same spirit in which I have striven to create and conduct it as a public institution, from motives higher than mere gain and it having been my desire that it should be at all times conducted in a spirit of independence and with a view of inculcating high standards and public spirit among the people and their official representatives."

According to Denis Brian, Pulitzer expected his three sons—Ralph, Joe, and Herbert—to carry out his wishes regarding his prized New York paper. "Each had something of their

father's personality—Ralph his idealism, Joe his guts, Herbert his stubbornness—but none matched his incredible drive, curiosity, and intelligence."

In 1930, nineteen years after Joseph Pulitzer's death, the *New York World* was seriously struggling. Its circulation had plummeted and its competition was formidable. There were the new morning tabloids, such as the *Daily News*. There was also Adolph Ochs, who had reinvigorated the *New York Times*, and there was the freshly merged *Herald Tribune*.

Pulitzer's once all-powerful *World* seemed to be at a loss for how to position itself. After Pulitzer's death, it had briefly captured the public's attention as well as a devoted readership in the 1920s. This was under the aegis of an inspired editor, Herbert Bayard Swope, who filled its columns with writing by the likes of Walter Lippman and Haywood Broun. But after 1923, Ralph and Tony Pulitzer proved ill equipped to run the paper. For this, the critics blamed the father more than the sons.

According to Pulitzer's biographer James McGrath Morris, "As an absentee owner, Joseph had refused to cede sufficient control so that a corporate management structure could be built. The internal disunion at the paper was aggravated by his system of keeping his managers competing and spying on each other. Joseph had remained the keystone in the arch of management." With the coming of the Great Depression in 1929, the losses became insurmountable. The three brothers agreed to sell the *World* to Scripps-Howard on February 27, 1931, for five million dollars, after obtaining a judge's consent to break their father's stipulation that the newspaper never be sold.

By the time Tony Pulitzer died in 1957, the family coffers had been considerably depleted, and even though Tony's children, Patsy

and Peter, had been brought up in opulent style, they were quite taken aback by how different their actual inheritance was from their expectations. The Pulitzer Prize and the Pulitzer name were shining more brightly than ever, so a huge amount of money was instantly conjured up in people's imaginations by the name; however, the reality was quite different. In a 1982 article in *People* magazine, Peter was said to have been left half a million dollars. One of Patsy's daughters once complained to a relative that Patsy was stunned to find that her father's will stipulated only two hundred thousand dollars for her.

Peter Pulitzer, Tony's son, was twenty-two when he married Lilly McKim. He had lost his mother, the former Gladys Munn Amory, when he was only seven years old.

Gladys had married Tony Pulitzer in 1926 after being recently divorced from flamboyant Palm Beach social figure Charles Amory, by whom she already had a son and a daughter. She soon bore Tony two exceptionally good-looking children: Patsy and Peter.

A slightly built, fashion-conscious, genuinely sweet woman, Gladys was related by blood to not only every prominent family in Palm Beach but to many leading families in the United States, from Philadelphia to Chicago to Sonoma, California. These families had made colossal fortunes as grain dealers, sugar merchants, tobacco farmers, and meatpackers as well as barons of railroads, shipping companies, and finance and included Armours, Astors, Biddles, Boardmans, Drexels, Gurnees, Orrs, Spreckels, Vanderbilts, and Wanamakers. It was an era when these people dominated their communities, and when they came together in Palm Beach during the winter months, they became practitioners of the good life on a scale incomparable to anything today.

For example, Florenz Ziegfeld and his actress wife, Billie Burke, who regularly vacationed in the Munns' place, would bring along their daughter's pair of pet lion cubs. When they left, their thank-you gift to their hosts was an orchestra that would play for seven nights in a row, during which the fun and fizz, the partying and high jinks, would continue nonstop.

Gladys's brother, Charles Alexander Munn, a movie-star-handsome Harvard graduate, was known as Mr. Palm Beach. He was a founder of three of the Florida Gold Coast's most beautiful private social hubs: the Everglades Club, the Seminole Club, and the Gulfstream Golf Club. For more than six decades, this classically elegant man who sported a slim mustache was often called "the last gentleman," as he straddled both American high society and the international jet set. He is credited with popularizing the navy blue blazer, until then called a captain's jacket, as well as the silk foulard ascot as a substitute for a tie for elegant informal occasions.

Patsy Pulitzer Preston remembered the day when Peter, she, their half-brother Charles Amory Jr. and half-sister Grace Amory, their mother Gladys Pulitzer, and many of their Munn relatives were lined up in their white shoes in front of the Munn family seaside cottage at the Breakers Hotel in Palm Beach for a photograph. "My mother, Gladys Munn, was the most loving, most caring person in the world," Patsy explained. "She died of TB in 1938. My father's last years with my mother were spent traveling around the world trying to find a cure that did not exist. Because of the contagion and beliefs of the time, we were unable to be in the same room with her. Imagine never being able to see the person you love the most," she said with a sigh to Augustus Mayhew, author of *House of Munn: The Palm Beach Story.*

As Ogden Phipps had astutely surmised, Peter was reared by nannies in Palm Beach. Like his sister, Patsy, he attended and graduated from an exclusive New England boarding school,

St. Mark's in Massachusetts. Like Lilly, he was a college dropout. He had enrolled at Stanford University, instead of Harvard, where his father had hoped he would go, but after freshman year switched to the University of Virginia. A single semester in Virginia convinced him that school was not for him. He quit and went back to Palm Beach, where he soon found out that his father was in financial trouble, dodging creditors, even having trouble keeping the Palm Beach family property maintained.

At age twenty Peter borrowed a few thousand dollars and opened a liquor store. When he turned twenty-one, he inherited $110,000 from his grandfather's estate, with which he bought some vacant land along the Florida coast. This turned out to have been a smart investment, because when the U.S. government forced him to sell some of this land for its new superhighway project, the building of I-95, Peter made an enormous profit. He parlayed his five-hundred-thousand-dollar inheritance from his father into extending the liquor store into a bowling alley and turning the remaining coastal land into the Pulitzer Orange Grove and Packing Company. Then he ventured into ranching and some international holdings—in short, he was already on his way to building a multimillion-dollar business.

When Lilly married him, he was a local legend, a young entrepreneur who piloted his own plane to and from his Florida cattle ranches, his citrus groves, and his hotel developments in Miami. He was earthy and unafraid of the more primitive side of Florida. He was familiar with agricultural chemicals and fertilizers as well as with pruning and picking fruit. He spent his days rubbing shoulders with farmers and ranchers, picking up tips on animal bloodlines, and braving the swampy world inhabited by alligators and snakes.

Lanky and athletic, Peter was a neat dresser, comfortable in the preppy Bermuda colors that men wore at casual parties in the tropics. He was described by *Vanity Fair*'s Laura Jacobs as "think

Apollo Belvedere goes early *Esquire*." But there was a touch of the renegade in him. In those days it was unusual for a young man of his class to sport a two-inch tattoo on his right forearm—a tattoo of what in photographs looks like a prowling panther.

A risk-taking, rule-breaking romantic by nature, Lilly broke out of her sheltered childhood and luxe surroundings with her daring choice of a husband. Part of Peter's allure for Lilly, according to Susanna Cutts, a longtime Florida friend of Lilly's, is that there was something "needing a leap of faith" on her part for her to run away with him, to "run away from her own platinum spoon" existence.

When Peter called Lilly's father, Robert McKim, and announced, "I've just married your daughter," McKim asked, "Which one?" When Peter called her mother, Lillian Phipps, she was in the middle of a card game. He told her the news, then handed the phone to Lilly, who heard her mother exclaim, "My God, Lilly Lee has just gotten married." This made Lilly burst into tears. Years later she confessed in an interview that at the time of her elopement she really hadn't fully "thought about what marriage was." She had not considered all its weighty ramifications. "It was just my next adventure" is how she remembered it.

An adventure it was. Photographs attest to the undeniable attraction and love between the softly curvaceous, young Lilly, who is often portrayed tenderly wrapping an arm around the neck of the chiseled-featured, dark-haired, perpetually tanned outdoorsman, who at twenty-two was successful in his own right as a pioneer in rugged, unpredictable central Florida.

CHAPTER 8

Lillys Blooming Everywhere

WHEN THE BRIGHT AND CHEERFUL SHORT dresses hanging on the pipe rack next to the citrus stand began to outsell juiced oranges and grapefruits from his Indian River groves, Peter Pulitzer was every bit as amused and enthusiastic as Lilly was. "He was very proud of what was going on," Lilly acknowledged to freelance writer Lorna Koski in a *Sun Sentinel* article in 1989. Lilly added, "I just kept rolling. . . . I don't have a competitive bone in my body, but somehow he got me to compete. He was always great that way." More to the point, however, both husband and wife realized right away: "My God, we've got something!"

Friends, and friends of friends, began asking Lilly where the unique printed dress she was wearing came from and how they could buy one just like it. The first dozen "little nothing" dresses, as Lilly called them, intended just to keep herself cool and comfortable while bending down for the

fruit and squeezing the juice, flew off the rack; then the next batch of twenty knee-grazing, sleeveless shifts with side slits to allow for even more movement were similarly scooped up.

At that point, Lilly started buying fabric by the bagful. The cotton for these mostly came from the five-and-dime, and their prints were mostly colored in the practical stain-hiding and dribble-proof hues of lemon yellow, lime green, and grapefruit pink.

The third batch, which really did begin to outsell the fruit, was different. Flashes of what would delight the eye and a calculation of what would actually sell started to dominate Lilly's choices. Beside the usual functional palette of citrusy yellows, greens, and pastel pinks, she found herself attracted to red-and-white-checked gingham—fabric meant for making kitchen curtains. She imagined it as perfect for one of her increasingly shorter and bolder, scrubbed and innocent-looking, cotton shifts that resembled children's play dresses. She envisioned it falling easily and simply over any female body, redefining it into a jaunty geometric shape. The secret of its clear-cut distinctiveness had to be the quality of the muslin lining. Lilly concluded that she had to have another talk with her Swiss dressmaker.

And so the Lilly Pulitzer fashion trademark of cool elegant ease originated. She also saw these merrily printed dresses as potential decorative art—like freestanding sculpture or haphazard wall hangings, enhancing the atmosphere of her juice bar.

The first to fall head over heels in love with the gingham dress was Lilly's boarding school friend, Jackie Kennedy. By this time the First Lady bought a dress off Lilly's rack and the next day wore it to Lilly's house, spoon-feeding little John-John on Lilly's kitchen floor. Although most of the dresses Lilly was selling cost between twenty-five and forty-five dollars at this time, Lilly charged Jackie seventy-five dollars for hers, "because that was

made out of very expensive curtain fabric," Lilly told Sarah Haight in a 2008 interview in *W* magazine. Haight wrote, "The unlikely designer's fame was all but cemented a year later, when . . . first lady Jackie Kennedy appeared in *Life* magazine wearing the Lilly Pulitzer Classic Shift."

It was a remarkable photo: Jackie's bare tanned legs and sandal-clad feet dangled from beneath the red-and-white slit hem as the leader of the free world was shown relaxing with his attractive wife and children against the railing of a white-framed Hyannis Port porch, with the Atlantic sparkling in the background. It was as American as apple pie and the Fourth of July. But it also gave the nation a glimpse of leisure at its civilized, upper-crust best.

Lilly likes to credit the confluence of timing and luck, as well as the place and the name, for her success. Her last name was familiar because of the Pulitzer Prizes; the time and the place were the fact that when the Lilly debuted, the Kennedy clan was vacationing not only on Cape Cod but also more often in Palm Beach.

Her business grew in the same impulsive, improvisational spirit in which it had begun. "Everything was fun and attractive and crazy. There was always music, always dancing," she remembers. Her customers were drinking juice, helping to squeeze oranges, and learning to do the twist. It was all casual and seemingly effortless. She never had an actual pattern for her dressmaker. Some of her dresses had armholes that were "only two inches wide," she laughingly claims, "but people's bodies are so weird, there was always a customer that had a tiny arm."

That Lilly had a private dressmaker, whom she probably shared with her mother and her sisters, was not at all unusual in the late

1950s. In those days dressmakers played an important role in most fashion-conscious American women's lives. Seventh Avenue was mass-producing plenty of appealing clothes, but most well-heeled, well-dressed women looked for wardrobe inspiration outside the United States. This was before the explosion of luxurious ready-to-wear clothing as we know it today.

In New York, Indiana-born Bill Blass and Louisiana-bred Geoffrey Beene were just beginning to gain recognition as high-end designers. Calvin Klein, Donna Karan, and Ralph Lauren were not yet on the horizon. Discerning women who took pride in being ahead of the mainstream would clip photographs of coats, dresses, and evening gowns shown by French or Italian couturiers, then try to find a similar fabric and have an expert dressmaker faithfully reproduce the outfit to their exact personal measurements. It was a made-to-order system, used by those who could afford it.

Even Jacqueline Kennedy was brought up thinking that to be a pacesetter one had to look to Paris. Jackie's figure was similar to Audrey Hepburn's; in the 1950s and 1960s Hepburn was the fashion muse of leading French designer Hubert de Givenchy. The First Lady looked longingly to his Parisian collection for ideas while developing her own glamorous and imaginative signature style.

The clothes Jackie favored during the Camelot years captivated the nation and the world. Ultimately, she became the twentieth century's most legendary fashion icon. During her husband's presidency she patriotically hired an American, Oleg Cassini, to be her exclusive designer, but it emerged later that she secretly asked Cassini to tailor her special-occasion outfits along Givenchy's exquisitely pared-down and soigné sculpted lines.

Jackie wasn't the first high-profile woman to wear Lilly's little dresses. Dina Merrill and Happy Rockefeller were the first prominent high-society women to sport Lilly shifts. But in the

1960s, especially during the brief period of the Kennedy years, nothing popularized the Lilly more than the fact that Jackie Kennedy and her sisters-in-law, Ethel and Joan Kennedy, as well as little Caroline and the president's mother, Rose—all different ages and entirely different female figure types—were spotted looking equally fresh and breezy in the colorful prints while shopping on Worth Avenue in Palm Beach.

Suddenly Lilly's shifts took off in a really big way. Pretty soon, every woman in Palm Beach wanted the garment they began to call a Lilly. And the fact that many of these stylish women had second homes quickly spread interest in the Lilly to points north—especially to Massachusetts resorts like Nantucket, and Martha's Vineyard—and to the country clubs of Nashville, Grosse Pointe, and Greenwich.

Everyone was clamoring for more. By 1961 people were indeed coming more for the shifts than the juice, and Lilly decided it was time to make dresses full-time.

Around this time Lilly met Laura Pyzel Robbins, who had been a fashion editor at *Harper's Bazaar* under Diana Vreeland, according to a friend of both Lilly and Laura's, Eve Hatch Holmes, the fashion director of *Bazaar*'s sister magazine at Hearst, *Town & Country*, during the 1950s and 1960s.

A New York friend of Lilly's sister Memsie, Laura had just moved to Florida because her husband, William Robbins, had been transferred by Merrill Lynch to head the firm's office in the Palm Beach area. At Memsie's urging, Laura telephoned Lilly and offered to help. "Lilly—with her three little children and numerous dogs, and don't forget the monkey, never really having worked before, not to speak of running a demanding, fast-growing clothes business before—had some hesitation, definite concerns about how to take the necessary next steps," Holmes

recalls. "She didn't have a clue about how the fashion industry worked. Whereas Laura, having been at *Harper's Bazaar* for years, knew all the ropes. She knew heads of department stores. She knew all sorts of influential fashion folk. Laura was a godsend to her at this stage of the game."

When they met over lunch, Lilly confided to Laura that it made her nervous that every night when Peter arrived home from the orange groves, the first thing he'd say to Lilly was, "Well, what have you done about the shop?" Peter had been after her for some time to open a real shop. The little clothes rack next to the stand no longer sufficed to hold the merchandise on demand. But with the upcoming resort season, Peter also saw another opportunity for temptingly displaying gift boxes and taking orders for selectively picked and packed fruit from the groves. He decided it was high time to end selling on the street. So one day he took it upon himself to rent a shop, shaded by striped awnings and cascading bougainvillea, in a pretty little alley, Via Mizner, behind Worth Avenue.

The Via Mizner shop had a wonderful color-splashed ambience. Lilly stamped her personality on the space despite the fact that its official name was the Pulitzer Groves Fruit Shop. Her flagship boutique showcased her ability to marry eclectic elements and to blend worldliness with coziness. Her vivid candy-colored dresses dominated the place, hanging against a wallpaper of yellow and orange daisies and stuck into circular bamboo racks resembling airy Panamanian birdcages.

The inviting, quirky, tropical extravaganza was further achieved with huge Mexican paper flowers, potted orchids, Russian matryoshka dolls, and baskets of cellophaned grapefruit, oranges, and kumquats poised on a wooden wheelbarrow as if about to samba on the head of Carmen Miranda. Dangling white beads of various shapes and sizes served as curtains. They were matched by a white wrought-iron sleigh bed strewn with pillows

in the same exuberant fabrics as the dresses. The sleigh bed provided an informal seating arrangement and emphasized Lilly's fashion message of multicolor prints.

"Lilly was great at the fun part, the creative part—she was both instinctively practical and artistically original," Holmes observes. "She knew what she liked, what colors and patterns worked together; what dress should have short sleeves, cap sleeves, or no sleeves; what should have a round neck or a boatneck or a V-neck; what should have a slit, what should be outlined in white piqué, and where a perky little bow could add just the right fillip. Basically she took the chemise—the sack dress, as it used to be called when Balenciaga introduced it—and she shortened and shaped it. Then she slit the side seams, which gave it a young feeling, a kick, and a sense of proportion the sack itself never had. Then, because she claimed she hated to wear underwear in the Florida heat, she added these perfect muslin linings, which gave both a nifty shape to the garment and kept you cool and comfy and airy—nothing sticking to your body underneath."

Holmes has a distinct appreciation for the humor of the absurd. Her father, Eric Hatch, wrote the *New Yorker* short story "1101 Park Avenue," which became the classic 1930s Carole Lombard screwball comedy *My Man Godfrey*. Holmes likes to tell a story of running into Lilly and Laura one day in the lobby of the Colony Hotel in Palm Beach. Jumping up with gusto at the sight of her two friends together, the next thing she knew, Lilly's rhesus monkey, Gooney, had taken a bite out of her ankle. "But to my amazement and chagrin," Holmes recalls, "no one seemed to take me seriously when in hysterical city-woman fashion I commanded the staff to instantly bring me iodine, Band-Aids, or still better, a doctor and some bandages."

Laura Robbins, today Laura Clark and living in Cuernavaca, Mexico, remembers being immediately struck by Lilly's "total command of scale and color." She volunteered to help Lilly cope

with the rapidly expanding fashion venture as well as with the operation of the boutique, where, she recounts, every day the two of them were up to their elbows in juice and pulp. The two women became partners ("foxhole buddies," Laura calls it), although no contract was signed.

Laura was a fashion expert, whereas Lilly, in her own words, "never cared a fig" for fashion—she had not had to deal with manufacturing, marketing, or shipping responsibilities before. Laura was familiar with how the retail seasons worked—when the delivery dates for spring, summer, cruise wear, or resort wear had to be met. In addition to knowing the heads of department stores, she personally knew many of the powerful buyers at upscale specialty stores throughout the United States and had a collegial relationship with many members of the fashion press in New York, with whom she would regularly sit at fashion shows.

Originally, all dresses in the shop sold for $22.50, an arbitrary price that Lilly and Laura came up with. To Laura's astonishment, there was a daily stampede for these cheaply priced shifts by women decked out in the costliest of jewels.

Polly Mellen, a legendary fashion editor who once merited a profile in the *New Yorker*, had been a major fashion arbiter and star at both *Harper's Bazaar* and *Vogue* magazines for decades. She was also a longtime friend of Lilly and Laura's. In 1959, she says, "Lilly's shifts were exploding, but only with a certain crowd. I'm talking about Palm Beach . . . the Everglades Club, the Bath & Tennis Club . . . Hobe Sound, which today is called the Jupiter Island Club." In these places, Mellen said, "Lilly and Laura launched a genuine status symbol."

"Laura knew more than I did—that's for sure," Lilly conceded in a 2003 *Vanity Fair* article, "Palm Beach's Barefoot Princess." Laura had been at *Harper's Bazaar* for years and had seen first-hand the most fastidiously executed seams and dressmaking details by the world's greatest masters of both haute couture and

ready-to-wear, and she thought that the original shifts were fine but a little amateurish. In an endearing but also tongue-in-cheek tone Laura would sometimes slip into calling the simple printed garments those "little rags."

"The line wasn't very extensive," Lilly admits. "Two bodies, one was sleeveless and one had sleeves. I mean everybody had to have them. Whether it fit or not, who cared? Just get one, I want it, I have to wear it to dinner."

Everyone in Palm Beach was already referring to these early dresses as a "Lilly" or the "Lilly shift," and, in fact, many of the conical or bell-shaped versions actually looked like an upside-down lily, but what to label the popular "little nothings" became an issue. Although by now Lilly had hired eighteen Cuban seamstresses from West Palm Beach and invested two thousand dollars in the enterprise, she didn't particularly want her name on the garments.

"I don't want publicity," she told Laura. The previous existence of another darling Lilly in the fashion business, the famous milliner Lilly Daché, plus the fact that the Indiana-based giant pharmaceutical firm Eli Lilly's philanthropic arm was an entity well known as the Lilly Foundation were also viewed by Lilly's team as potentially problematic roadblocks to registering Lilly as a brand name.

For a while the two women flirted with calling the line Lilly-Laura, but after some debate of the pros and cons, they concluded that almost everybody in the United States was somewhat acquainted with the name Pulitzer. "Let's call it Lilly Pulitzer," Laura is quoted as suggesting in the *Vanity Fair* article by Laura Jacobs.

In the initial stages of designing the dresses, Lilly would incorporate her first name somewhere in the pattern of the printed fabric—a sort of lyrical signature that was part of a twig, the petal of a blossom, or the wing of an insect. These earliest

dresses were made of 100 percent cotton and had metal zippers. According to the Vintage Fashion Guild, by the mid-1960s Lilly had started using a 65 percent polyester and 35 percent cotton blend that took especially well to absorbing the dyes for her ever busier, ever more color-drenched shifts, which had nylon zippers.

For a while the labels on the dresses were sewn inside and were marked THE LILLY with instructions that said HAND WASH ONLY. DO NOT DRYCLEAN. Today her registered trademark label consists of a large LILLY in a slightly left-leaning script over a small PULITZER in block letters. Lilly also began to use a very pretty, special hem lace, with her name spelled out through the holes of the lace-work's delicate white thread.

Lilly's first designs in pure cotton were produced by an Italian mom-and-pop operation in a family garage on the outskirts of Miami, near the Hialeah racetrack. The track was famous for its stunning central oval full of live pink flamingos, around which the world's finest thoroughbred horses competed during the winter months before Kentucky's springtime Bluegrass Stakes in Lexington and the Kentucky Derby in Louisville.

With the popularity of her clothes business growing exponentially, Lilly soon established her Miami sewing factory at 29th Avenue and 34th Street. According to the promotional brochure for the 2010–2011 exhibit "For the Love of Lilly," organized by the Museum of Lifestyle and Fashion in Boynton Beach, Florida, in celebration of fifty years of Lillys, Lilly Pulitzer Inc. would eventually have "450 employees that had a positive economic impact on the town of Palm Beach, Palm Beach County, and the State of Florida." She had "helped to create jobs along with defining an American preppy look and imbedding the combination of pink and green as official colors of Palm Beach."

Between 1945 and 1960, the rise of Florida as a major producer of the clothing it had been instrumental in pioneering and popularizing was a genuine source of wonder to the rest of the clothing industry. In the two decades after World War II, the Miami area became the third largest manufacturer of leisure wear and sportswear in the United States. This became a key component of the city's postwar economic boom.

That South Florida, in the span of such a short time, came to dominate the inspiration, development, and production of leisure clothes speaks volumes about the social and cultural changes that occurred in the region in the middle of the twentieth century. The Works Progress Administration's *Guide to Florida*, published in 1939 as part of Franklin D. Roosevelt's Federal Writers Project, is a revealing portrait of a state still in the Depression and yet to be rescued by the infusion of federal money. It was a sleepy place, with only about a million souls from Key West to Pensacola, unrecognizable from today's heavily developed behemoth of fourteen million people.

The growth of the fashion industry around Miami reflects the maturation of the southern tip of the state. Palm Beach provided the initial impetus. From the beginning, with its tropical flora and exotic fauna, it promised unfettered year-round adventure to budding sportsmen with the financial wherewithal and the urge for travel. Those seeking luxurious recreation looked to South Florida resorts, especially the island of Palm Beach, as their private playgrounds. They needed play clothes, and because of who they were, their upper-echelon preferences in what to wear for sailing, tennis, and golf—clothes and accessories often bought in England or France—influenced how the rest of the mainstream United States dressed for its favorite activities away from the workplace.

Perhaps the most important boon to Lilly Pulitzer's business, as she needed to produce more merchandise, was finding just the right people to help create the fabrics. It was through a ceramic artist friend, Franci Young, that Lilly was introduced to Peter Pell and Jimmy Russell, an openly gay couple who were both émigrés from Broadway's theater world and who had fallen under the spell of Florida's southernmost city, Key West. They had recently founded a "hand-screening, hand-printing, hand-blocking, hand-everything" business called Key West Hand Printing Fabrics.

Suddenly, everything Lilly dreamed of and needed to accomplish seemed to have materialized. It turned out to be an ideal collaboration. The result was a madcap technicolor tropicana of Pulitzer prints: swinging monkeys, giant peapods, dancing daiquiri glasses, bursting blooms, wingspread butterflies, and sea horses and seashells bumping into each other in the wildest jamboree of almost psychedelic tints.

Lilly's palette was clear and clean. It was as intensely colorful as a Peter Max poster, but the print motif was never blurred, muddy, or hippie-ish. The wild Pulitzer color mixes had a fresh, precise effect, an air of mischievous innocence that echoed the protected fun and frolic of boarding school days. Every fabric, not just the famous original pink-and-green combination, had a preppy feel to it from the very start. "It was a total change of life for me," Lilly recalled to *W* magazine's Sarah Haight about the time she started her line. "I entered it with no business sense. . . . It was just something that I all of a sudden took over."

Soon she was regularly flying to Key West to meet with Pell and Russell, whose nascent textile business was also about to go into orbit. A couple of years later, their unique fabrics were among the unequivocal hit displays at the exciting New York Trade Fair of 1964. The Lilly Pulitzer fabrics turned out to be a marvelous conjunction of talents.

Pell was a former actor who had become a stage manager; he had worked with Rosalind Russell from 1956 to 1958 on the original Broadway production of *Auntie Mame*, with Tallulah Bankhead in a Tennessee Williams play, and with many other major theatrical luminaries up to the summer of 1960. It was then, while vacationing with Jim Russell (no relation to Rosalind), who had also appeared in several Broadway shows and was a regular on television for a year, that the two of them succumbed to the charms of Key West, which lured them into seeking a means of living there permanently.

They pooled their artistic abilities and decided to produce handprints. They soon set up shop in a 125-year-old waterfront building that had housed Key West's first bank and furnished it with several sixty-yard-long printing tables on which fabric designs were hand screened. Pell became the art director and Russell was the sales manager. A February 1968 article in the *St. Petersburg Times* reported that they were soon joined by a third partner, Bill E. Johnson, who had administrative experience in the coal business in Tennessee and became treasurer.

Although all three partners were strangers to the textile industry, they plunged right in, and soon they were successfully hand-printing tea towels. Within a very short time, they were producing a sizable collection of riveting and unusual prints, thematically inspired by the Florida Keys. Escalating demand for these serigraphs on the finest Sea Island cotton—that is, original color prints made by pressing pigments, mostly natural dyes, through a silk screen with a stencil design—prompted them to hire another designer.

So they brought in Key West artist Suzie Zuzek dePoo, who was making a name for herself locally with her intricate representational watercolors of floral, landscape, and seascape imagery that reflected the natural beauty of the Keys. Today an octogenarian and perhaps the most venerated of several famous female artists of Key West, Suzie was classically trained, which had perfectly

prepared her for the task at hand. She had graduated from the Pratt Institute in New York on the G.I. Bill after serving in World War II.

Even though she continued to have gallery exhibits of her watercolors, ceramic tile creations, and shaped and painted-on works from driftwood and centuries-old reclaimed glass from Bottle Beach, she soon became the full-time head fabric designer of the company. She stayed on for the next thirty years, during which time she brought in two more designers: her daughter, Martha dePoo, and Leigh Martin Hooten.

Suzie's series of fabric designs attracted Lilly's interest. Lilly's first step was to send her sister Memsie to reconnoiter. When Memsie returned from Key West with a fistful of enchanting swatches and uncurbed enthusiasm, repeatedly saying, "You can't believe it," Lilly herself hopped over by plane, and the creative synergy that resulted in the famous Pulitzer prints was forged.

Together Lilly and Suzie dreamed up brilliant-green palm trees, blown-up sunflowers, and shocking pink gardenias, all plucked from their collective sun-dappled lives. Lilly would arrive in Key West at regular intervals with long lists of leafy and flowering plants, whimsical animals in unexpected situations, and suggestions of color schemes that future prints would incorporate. There was always a lot of laughter, especially while naming the prints.

These powwows could turn quite naughty. For example, a print motif of panda bears playing with beach balls was called BearBalls. Lilly, Peter, Jimmy, and Suzie also came out with some erotic prints, which may or may not have been made into Lilly Pulitzer shifts. In any case, they were sold under the counter to delighted personal friends.

"I was always on the road, bouncing around and happy," Lilly told Larissa MacFarquhar, in a 2000 "Annals of Style" piece in the *New Yorker*. "It was so fun you can't believe it. I spent three or four days every week in the factory, I couldn't tear myself out of

there. What a blast! Yanking out those bolts to decide what was going into what—oh, God! It was all just like a fairy tale."

Laura Robbins would occasionally accompany Lilly on the flights to Key West on Peter Pulitzer's two-engine Navion plane. On one of these jaunts, the plane crashed into shark-infested waters 28 miles after taking off from the Key West airport, on a return flight to West Palm Beach 150 miles away over open water. Whether the pilot, who was not Peter but a woman named Alicia Cuomo, forgot to refuel or the engines simply failed is not known. The plane made a pancake landing into about ten feet of water approximately eight miles northwest of the original Bahia Honda Bridge. Lilly suffered a concussion and was bleeding from the head after she was thrown through the glass window of the plane, and she managed to scramble onto the wing of the partly submerged plane.

The Pulitzer plane's distress signal was picked up by a South Central Airlines plane and relayed to the Key West naval station. Nevertheless, Laura and Lilly became increasingly fearful that rescuers might not be able to spot them because it was already dusk and the sky was rapidly darkening over the wreckage. So the instant they sighted the navy helicopter approaching, Laura quickly zipped out of her bright orange Lilly shift and frantically began waving the dress in the air to get the attention of the helicopter pilot. Looking at topless Laura and relieved to be plucked off the wing of the plane by the chopper, Lilly saw the humor in it all, despite being somewhat dazed and bleeding seriously. "Tits will get 'em every time," she quipped.

Within a year Lilly was shipping orders to retailers including Lord & Taylor and Saks Fifth Avenue and also to now defunct prestigious stores like Nan Duskins in Philadelphia and I. Magnin in San Francisco. She didn't allow the stores to order specific

patterns; the clothes would arrive as a surprise. "I don't know how to explain what it was like to run my business, the joy of every day," she reminisced to Laura Jacobs in *Vanity Fair*. "I got a kick every time I went into the shipping department. I had to pat [the dresses] on the box and kiss them. I loved seeing them going out the door. I loved selling them in the shop. I liked them on the body. Everything. There's no explaining the fun I had."

But the first order shipped to Lord & Taylor—an important break for Lilly into a major market—turned out to be a disaster. Because the manufacturer had used a cheaper fabric, the linings shrank. "Here the business is just beginning," Lilly remembers thinking, "and it's going to end the same day." So she withdrew thirty thousand dollars from her trust and recalled the dresses. She had all the faulty linings cut out and put in new ones and sent the dresses out again. Lord & Taylor sold thousands of them.

The firm was set up. Lilly became president, Peter became vice president, and Laura became secretary-treasurer. An absolutely frantic period for all three followed. Not only did they have to produce a lot more clothes for an "I've got to have it" clientele, but the whole corporate angle also had to be attended to. Legal matters were looming. The company was selling Lillys like mad, and some styles were already being knocked off by competitors before Lilly had gotten a registered trademark, before the unique fabrics had been copyrighted, and before the boutique or possible future boutiques had been officially registered.

Laura was indispensable during this early period. Blond and lovely, she too was from a wealthy family; her father had been the head of Dun & Bradstreet's vast Latin American operations. Laura was an asset to Lilly in every way. She was always up-to-date in the way she looked because she had been trained through her magazine experience to be instinctively abreast of the latest trends. Although she and her husband lived in Boca Raton, about thirty miles away, she was always ready to contact

her friends at *Harper's Bazaar* about some fashion or publicity fine point, ready to turn to retailers she knew about merchandising and advertising procedures. She understood both the fickle nature of fashion and how to keep the mystique of a winner going.

Laura remembers the energy and gaiety that went into spinning variations on the theme of the original Lilly garment. "Lilly was gung-ho a hundred percent," she says. "Four hundred percent!" she corrects herself. "Very smart, and [with] the stamina of ten men."

The two women didn't pay themselves wages but put all of the profit right back into the company. Bookkeeping was erratic. If an invoice was mystifying or too complicated, it was just pushed into a corner, and sometimes almost forgotten, until an irate person demanded that it be followed up on.

In June 1962, Lilly journeyed to Manhattan to sign a contract for nationwide distribution of her shifts and got an order from Henri Bendel. On Christmas Eve 1962, President John F. Kennedy nearly bought out the store. By this time, Lilly Pulitzer products had been designed for an entire family. Her smart shifts were replicated for little girls and called "the Minnie" after one of Lilly's daughters. A clever marketing move included swimming trunks, ties, and trousers for men as well as a cotton nightshirt dubbed the "Sneaky Pete" after her husband. "It seemed fitting," she commented years later. During the height of the 1961–1962 resort season alone, *Time* magazine reported, sixteen hundred Lillys were grabbed up in Palm Beach.

What changed everything and catapulted Lilly Pulitzer from a local phenomenon into a national celebrity was a sensational photo essay in *Life* magazine in February 1963. At the time, *Life* was the most popular general-interest magazine in the country,

with the largest circulation, and Laura had a lot to do with making the story happen. Sally Kirkland, mother of the actress with the same name, was one of the three most influential voices of the era's fashion media (the other two were the imperious Diana Vreeland and the tiny and sharp Eugenia Sheppard). Kirkland put together an all-time knockout series of layouts on Lilly, an eight-page story titled "A Barefoot Tycoon Makes Lillies Bloom All Over."

Although people were beginning to hear about her label, Lilly had never been in a major magazine before. With her brown eyes; dark tresses piled high; pretty, upturned nose; and shapely long legs, she was a very photogenic subject. Though publicity shy, she came across as an exotic but dynamic beauty living a charmed and exuberant tropical life. She was pictured in various scenes: sailing on the *Vergemer*, a 118-foot diesel yacht belonging to her mother and her stepfather; working in her spectacularly technicolor Via Mizner shop; and dashing from her husband's plane hugging rolls of fabric under one arm while he, still in the pilot's seat, admiringly looked at the way her dress flipped open at the sides and showed off her legs.

Despite the fact that Laura was a good friend of Sally Kirkland's and had suggested the story idea to her, when it came time to do the *Life* magazine photo shoot, Kirkland completely ignored Laura and put the entire focus on Lilly in her Lillys. Laura was never mentioned in the article. Her feelings were hurt, and even though the two partners eventually split on a friendly note, from that day on it was clear to everyone, including Lilly, that Lilly Pulitzer Inc. was solely hers.

When the article in *Life* appeared, two more Lilly Pulitzer boutiques had already opened in Florida besides the original one in Palm Beach. The others were located in Boca Raton and Naples; the former was managed by Laura until she and her husband

moved to Santa Barbara, California. A couple of years later, Lilly bought out Laura's share of the company in a settlement that satisfied both.

The records indicate that these first three boutiques were incorporated under the Florida State Department of Agriculture and listed in the Division of Fruit and Vegetable Inspection Commission's Annual Report of 1963. Presumably, the gift baskets of oranges and grapefruit sold in Lilly's shops account for this. Also in 1963, Lilly opened her first boutique up north, in Edgartown, Massachusetts, on Martha's Vineyard.

Shrewdly and kindly, Lilly launched her boutiques in the communities to which her friends moved when their husbands were transferred because of their jobs. These were usually wealthy locales like Palm Desert and La Jolla, California; Bloomfield Hills, Michigan; and Watch Hill, Rhode Island. She thought these uprooted wives needed something to do. But sometimes she did it because a friend truly needed a job to support herself and her family. At the company's peak in the late 1960s and the early 1970s, Lilly Pulitzer boutiques had popped up all across the country, not just along seashores but inland and in the heartland, numbering nearly three dozen and generating an estimated fifteen million dollars in revenue.

Modestly, Lilly would occasionally protest that she was not a true fashion designer. "I can't cut, I can't sew, I don't draw." Yet the consensus of the fashion press was that the nondesign of the Lilly was its allure. The perky, color-imbued, and unpretentious shift in cotton met an American need for personal style in the midst of a homogeneous culture.

In her 1967 bestselling book, *The Beautiful People*, Marylin Bender quoted Lilly as saying, "The great thing about the Lilly is that you wear practically nothing underneath."

When asked whether Lilly's famously quoted insistence that she didn't wear anything under her Lilly was true or false, her

friend Eve Holmes just raised her eyebrows and shrugged. But in its simple wearability and the simplicity of the garment's shape and its bold tropical print, Lilly understood the time she lived in as much as she understood herself.

The late 1950s and the early 1960s, when the Lilly made its first big splash on the fashion scene, were postwar years full of vitality and optimism, marked by a confidence in progress and a respect for taste. There was a general bursting forth of color. Color was everywhere: through advances in color film, the increased printing of color pages in magazines, the sudden profusion of Technicolor movies, and breakthroughs in methods of printing brighter fabrics (cleaner dyes and improved fabrics that were better at accepting these newer brilliant dyes).

Then came the emergence of pop art and op art through the genius of artists including Frank Stella, Victor Vasarely, and Andy Warhol. In Italy, Emilio Pucci was introducing never-before-seen kaleidoscopic prints on brazen geometric-patterned silk jerseys that clung to the figure in sensual ways. And in Finland, bold combinations of red, pink, and orange in big blown-up abstract graphics on stiff cotton Marimekko fabrics swung away from the body in tentlike dresses that were eye-catching and carefree.

Lilly's sense of uplifting color was in tune with this changing aesthetic climate, as whims that were once elite evolved into mass phenomena. Lilly also changed merchandising by extending the resort season in fashion to virtually the whole year. When told by one retailer that she had to make fall and winter clothes, she replied, "Oh, but you don't understand, it's always summer somewhere."

CHAPTER 9

The Perpetual Party Town

ONCE THERE WERE FOUR SEASONS, which were as clearly marked in the fashion world as elsewhere, but now there is a fifth, the Palm Beach season," noted the *New York Times.* This quote is not from the early 1960s, when a barely thirty-year-old Palm Beach–based designer transfixed the fashion world with her special decorative prints on simple and utilitarian shapes, with a growing coterie of fans aged seven to seventy. The *Times* observation was made in the Roaring Twenties, a decade in which socialites, society columnists, moviemakers, fashion magazines, manufacturers, and retailers regularly referred to "the Palm Beach season" and the necessity of a "Palm Beach wardrobe."

Lilly has always said that the fantasy island from which she vaulted to fame played an integral part in her success. Now, in the twenty-first century, Lilly Pulitzer is deservedly considered the Doyenne of the Palm Beach Look, as the

Museum of Lifestyle and Fashion History in Boynton Beach, Florida, referred to her in 2011.

From as early as 1900, the cultural cachet of what was worn in Palm Beach by day and by night had a resounding impact on the U.S. fashion scene at large. According to costume historians Richard Martin and Harold Koda, at some point "Palm Beach became a colloquial reference." The town's name itself became a catchall term for luxe leisure clothing and novel sportswear.

In time it would be the pink-and-green, magenta-and-yellow, peach-and-turquoise shift dresses, golf skirts, bikinis, men's jackets, and men's trousers launched by Lilly Pulitzer that would be known the world over as mainstays of the Palm Beach look. Today these items color the collective imagination about the resort. Emblematic of this in-the-know style that exudes sportive grace and joie de vivre are, along with the Pulitzer "must-haves," pastel-colored, crocodile-emblazoned Lacoste polo shirts; Ralph Lauren Polo cable-knit sweaters, preferably tossed and tied over the shoulders; subtle gold-chain necklaces and gold bangle bracelets and Stephen Bonanno sandals for women; and for men sockless dark loafers from Gucci or from John Lobb, England's bespoke shoemaker made world famous as James Bond's choice of footwear.

Although these casual fashion items became country-club classics across the United States during the past half century of eased formalities, they still reverberate with their origins as status uniforms in the stunning tropical paradise where the nation's rich and famous flock to play, give opulent balls, and occasionally do wicked things that make sensational news. All of the above have fascinated people from the time the resort was founded.

The name *Palm Beach* came about because the place was exactly that: a long sandy beach with tall palm trees on it. Although the beach had been there from the beginning, the coconut palms

were not indigenous to the island. They "arrived from the sea in startlingly appropriate fashion," wrote John Ney in *Palm Beach: The Place, the People, Its Pleasures and Palaces.* "If the story of Palm Beach is a fairy tale, the origins of the palms is a perfect beginning containing all the elements of later life: alcohol, confusion, an interminable party, visitors from elsewhere, a dubious project, and the weather. Tradition was established in poetic clarity and economy, and the future prefigured in primitive simplicity."

The Spanish Party, as old-timers proudly refer to the outlandish event resulting in the planting of fourteen thousand coconuts in the sand, began on January 9, 1879. A Spanish schooner called the *Providencia*, bound from Havana harbor for Barcelona with a mixed cargo of hides, wine, and coconuts, ran aground on the beach in a storm. The local pioneers were a dour lot from Illinois, led by William Lainhart and impelled to come by the Homestead Act of 1862.

Disheartened by their trying years in the hot wilderness along the untamed Florida shore of the settlement they called Lake Worth, they rushed to greet the stranded sailors and the disoriented captain of the ship. The pioneers, who had no regular source of strong drink, happily accepted the captain's nearly limitless offer of wine to celebrate his crew's survival. Thus began the first big recklessly extended beach party on the island, which foreshadowed more than a century of excessive nonstop partying and wild fun on the same spot.

At one point, the captain mentioned the twenty thousand coconuts he was carrying and offered them to his hosts. "Only at a large, noisy drinking session would twenty thousand coconuts seem tempting, desirable, and, finally, irresistible. And then only to unworldly pioneers anxious to break the monotony of their lives on any pretext," commented Ney. Besotted by days and nights of wine drinking, the laughing, shoving, and frequently falling-down settlers went as far as hauling fourteen thousand

coconuts off the ship and, in the next few days, planting them from one end of the wilderness beach to the other.

The Spanish crew was eventually picked up by another passing ship, but the local merrymakers, in Puritan fashion, were for years embarrassed to talk about the legendary Spanish Party. That it had actually taken place was attested to by the many palm trees pushing up through the earth a year or so later.

It was not until the early 1890s that the tremendous young palms were fully grown. Rising high among South Florida's low-lying scrubby landscape, these sheltering palms became recognized as the region's most beautiful asset. Softly rattling their graceful fronds in the tropical breeze, they seduced Standard Oil mogul Henry Morrison Flagler into building his resort of luxury and privilege there.

Since 1882, Flagler, the tycoon who began it all, had been casting about the lower end of the Florida peninsula for the ideal location for a superresort he wanted to build. Although Americans seeking outdoor recreation and invalids hoping for the health benefits of southern climes had already been frequenting Central Florida in those days, Flagler had another idea. "It occurred to me very strongly," he said at the time, "that someone with sufficient means ought to provide accommodations for that class of people who are not sick, but who come here to enjoy the climate, have plenty of money, but could find no satisfactory way of spending it." When at last Flagler set foot on the elongated piece of land surrounded by Lake Worth and the open Atlantic Ocean, he beheld the rugged marsh and brush and sand, but he was totally smitten by the palms. He saw not only what was there but also what could be there. He pronounced, "It shall be here and it shall be called Palm Beach." The rest is history.

Flagler was untiring in his determination to bring rich and powerful Americans' attention to the state's southern coasts. According to Deirdre Clemente, after Flagler developed the rail-road lines across a swampy jungle to ensure accessibility and erected the grand resorts to attract moneyed visitors, he and his hotels came to define South Florida as the perpetually sunny playground for the nation's upper echelon.

At the center of Flagler's empire, which included railroads, real estate, and newspapers, were the resplendent hotels of Palm Beach: the Royal Poinciana, built in 1894, which had its own ferry docks and mooring for pleasure craft, and the Palm Beach Inn, built in 1895, which was soon expanded and renamed the Breakers. According to Flagler's biographer, David Leon Chandler, "The success of Palm Beach was instant."

The purchase of the land for the sprawling wooden 1,150-room Royal Poinciana, the largest resort hotel in the world in its day, was widely publicized in newspapers and caused property values to skyrocket—from virtually no value at all to between $150 and $1,500 an acre, depending on the land's proximity to the Atlantic. Within a year, stellar members of the Social Register were developing walled estates along the seashore.

The topography of the island ensured exclusivity. At no point was it more than three-quarters of a mile wide, and at some places it was only five hundred feet (not even one-tenth of a mile) wide. Philadelphia's elite was the first to purchase property: the Wanamakers, the Stotesburys, and the Wideners arrived almost immediately. Other prosperous and prominent northerners soon followed. A guide to Florida published in the late 1930s called Palm Beach "the earthly Valhalla of financial achievement" and noted that it had long been regarded "as the winter counterpart of Newport."

As more hotel guests and homeowners arrived aboard their private railroad cars—among them, the Phippses—for the official

winter season, exclusive clubs with ten-thousand-dollar annual membership fees flourished. The names and hometowns of the new arrivals were published in the weekly paper, *Palm Beach Life.* The small stretch of sand became, as historian Larry R. Youngs wrote, "the icon of conspicuous consumption for America's upper classes."

In such an environment, fashion took center stage, and the demand for appropriate clothing was a constant concern. As *Vogue* magazine sympathized back in the late twenties, "Not to have the right clothes at Palm Beach is a tragedy. One feels duty bound to dress for an audience all the time." From the beginning, what was worn in Palm Beach influenced trends at other U.S. resorts. An advertisement for Wanamaker's department store in 1900 read, "Palm Beach is the style prophecy of Newport." Yet the clothing styles of Palm Beach were not native born. The ad continued: "Florida reflects the Riviera."

Concurrent with the ascent of Palm Beach was the rise of the French designer for Americans. By World War I, Paris-based fashion houses such as Paquin, Lanvin, and Worth were creating designs specifically intended for a Palm Beach clientele. So while Palm Beach had a long tradition as a place where styles were set, it was not the place where styles were made. Not until Lilly came along in the 1960s with her thrilling printed clothing did Palm Beach become a place where a new style was actually born.

From the start Lilly resisted having to make cold-weather clothes. She also avoided the big seasonal showcases for U.S. designers in New York. She staged her own shows and special events in her various boutiques, where she would regularly introduce her latest asymmetric floor-length evening dresses, eyelet-trimmed tunics, halter tops, capri pants, little girls' party dresses, and men's nightshirts. Occasionally she would show her latest line of designs at Palm Beach charity luncheons or cocktail benefits.

Whether consciously or unintentionally, Lilly was also ahead of her time in the way that she and her husband, Peter, burnished

the brand by associating it with their refreshingly natural and enviable Palm Beach lifestyle. It was a way of life that looked effortless yet was infinitely glamorous.

The sexual heat between the tropically clad Lilly and Peter radiated through their body language in article after article about them in *Sports Illustrated*, *Town & Country*, *Vogue*, and *Palm Beach Life*, which followed the *Life* magazine piece by Sally Kirkland. These stories opened a window on a world of seemingly offhand opulence where lives were utterly at ease with taste and beauty among jungle greenery and ocean waves, yachts and seaplanes, orchids and bougainvillea, crystalline swimming pools and pristine tennis courts, and attractively set luncheon tables with fit and tanned young men and women sitting around them sipping bloody bulls and piña coladas.

The Pulitzers embodied the elusive American upper-class comfort and cool so poignantly alluded to in F. Scott Fitzgerald's *The Great Gatsby*. Gatsby, the self-conscious outsider trying to penetrate high society, studies with awe the utter naturalness with which nattily dressed young men lean against their prized Jazz Age automobiles and slide behind the wheels of their velvet-upholstered Bugattis in Long Island.

A modest minister's son from upstate New York, Henry Morrison Flagler became a partner of John D. Rockefeller, but it was his all-consuming passion for making Palm Beach into the balmy pleasure dome of his dreams at which he most phenomenally succeeded. In some respects, Flagler was not unlike Lilly: he found his focus and went about it his own way. It was in response to his wife's fragile health that he looked to mild climates and thereby turned a hostile swamp into a landscape of luxury.

On March 14, 1896, the Florida East Coast Railroad, which would ultimately extend from Jacksonville to Key West and boast

a chain of elegant resort hotels from St. Augustine south, arrived in Palm Beach for the first time with a passenger list of the East Coast's most prominent social names. The moment brilliantly crowned Flagler's efforts. The train pulled right into a corner of the fabulously landscaped Royal Poinciana Hotel with its breathtaking Coconut Grove, a unique site for al fresco socializing, with hundreds of small tables and bamboo chairs invitingly scattered under the cooling shade of tall palm trees.

Out of Flagler's train stepped such leading Eastern Establishment types of the time as Cornelius and Alice Vanderbilt, Harry Payne Whitney, Lispenard Stewart, Thomas Cushing, Gertrude Vanderbilt, Edward Livingston, Dudley Winthrop, and Countess Gladys Vanderbilt Szechenyi.

Decade after decade, generation after generation, a glittering procession of people descended on the pedigreed preserve to enjoy their wealth. Starting with Flagler's own marble palace, Whitehall, which today is the Society of the Four Arts museum, more mansions of stunning extravagance rose along the island and became occupied by the families behind the nation's most phenomenal fortunes and best-known brand names.

By 1917, the gigantic seaside bastion, the Breakers Hotel, had become the number one perch of famous vacationers such as the legendary modern dancer Isadora Duncan and her multimillionaire lover, Paris Singer, one of eighteen illegitimate children of the inventor of the sewing machine. Singer eventually tired of Isadora and channeled all his energy into Palm Beach, building projects with a much-traveled and impoverished but colorful architect named Addison Mizner. Their first collaboration was the splendid Everglades Club, where Singer's eclectic collection of multicolored tiles from ruined buildings along the Mediterranean were incorporated in a manner Mizner had long fantasized about: a tropical palace of old-world style with a predominantly Spanish flavor.

And so the dominant look of Palm Beach was born. Bankrolled by Singer and designed by an ecstatic Mizner, the special architecture of the island was established. A critic at the time called Mizner's polyglot architectural style "Spanish—Moorish—Romanesque—Gothic—Renaissance—Bull Market—Damn the Expense."

The first of many women to be called "Queen of Palm Beach" to be bewitched by Mizner's Everglades Club was Eva Stotesbury. Known by the nickname Queen Eva or as "La Belle de Palm Beach," she was the flamboyant wife of Philadelphia financier Edward Stotesbury. "I simply love it," she exclaimed to her husband. "You must build me one." Mizner, a gigantic, three-hundred-pound man, was just waiting to be discovered, and when Stotesbury promised that she would spare no expense, the architect promptly ran for his sketch pad. According to *Palm Beach Babylon* by Murray Weiss and Bill Hofmann, she wanted:

> A mansion with panoramic views, a home large enough to hold twelve hundred guests at parties. Together Mizner and Queen Eva staked out a twenty-three-acre plot that ran the width of the island, from the Atlantic Ocean on the east to the estuary on the west. Mizner had the property cleared of jungle and in its center built a spectacular Mediterranean-style, thirty-seven-room villa, inspired by a convent near Burgos, Spain.

Again Mizner used Singer's antique tiles for dazzling decorative touches. He also installed enormous and extraordinary fireplaces. The ceilings were lofty. The windows were grated, and everything was built to invite a cross-current of soft breezes from the ocean and the lake. The estate had a private zoo, an open-air theater, and a spacious teahouse. The villa was called El Mirasol and it was filled with the largest private collection of art and antiques in the United

States. The moment the roof tiles were set, an opulent house-warming party for three hundred guests featured "champagne flowing like water" and "a buffet that never ran out."

In Philadelphia, Stotesbury, with her blazing showiness, was snubbed by a more conservative social oligarchy, but in Palm Beach many tried yet could not unseat her and her husband from the top of the social heap. It was not until 1927 that the Stotesbury mansion would be eclipsed by another.

Cereal heiress Marjorie Merriweather Post and her second husband, E. F. Hutton, built the incomparable 114-room Mar-a-Lago, until 2008 the Palm Beach property of Donald Trump, where he lavishly celebrated his third wedding on January 22, 2005, to the Slovenian beauty Melania Knauss, who wore a hundred-thousand-dollar Christian Dior gown twinkling with fifteen hundred hand-stitched crystals and pearls. The guest list included Hillary Clinton, Rudy Giuliani, Barbara Walters, and Simon Cowell, who feasted on the seven-tiered Grand Marnier chiffon wedding cake iced with three thousand cream roses.

As for El Mirasol, the Depression-era crashes took a terrific toll on its owners. Before the crash, Stotesbury, who was famous for her sparkling jewelry, used to rule over Palm Beach soirees wearing her famous knee-length strand of huge square emeralds that had once belonged to a czarina, and she even had two armed guards always standing by to protect the necklace. Now she had to have her opulent estate subdivided into six parcels. (Tony Pulitzer, Peter's father, was one of the first to buy a for-sale parcel. He purchased an acre of choice beachfront property for a hundred thousand dollars. He and five others built smaller homes on the glorious El Mirasol grounds. In time, the exorbitant maintenance costs caught up with the last owners of the ornate mansion, and in 1971, El Mirasol—where General Douglas

MacArthur had married his first wife, Louise, Eva Stotesbury's daughter, after defeating General John Pershing, his rival for her hand—was razed.)

Marjorie Post, a friendly rival of Eva's, and ultimately the most famous social figure other than Lilly to be associated with Palm Beach, lived in a manner totally different from the young designer of flowery shifts. Marjorie first visited Palm Beach in 1909, spending the winter at Flagler's wondrous Royal Poinciana Hotel. She was recuperating from back-to-back pregnancies and the difficult deliveries of her two daughters by her first husband, Edward Bennett Close, a lawyer from an established Greenwich family whose granddaughter is the actress Glenn Close.

By 1914, still in her twenties and an only child, Marjorie became one of the nation's wealthiest women through her inheritance. Her father was the ingenious entrepreneur C. W. Post, the inventor of the top-selling breakfast cereal Grape Nuts and the popular chicory-roasted cereal beverage Postum. Marjorie heeded her father's advice: "Don't be a miser and sit and count shekels. Money should be kept moving. Make it work. Make it create. Make it do good." She bought a sixty-six-room Fifth Avenue mansion and filled it with priceless Beauvais tapestries, Rubens paintings, and a treasure trove of antiques.

By this time World War I was under way, and her husband, a commissioned captain, went to France. Once the war had ended, Ed Close returned a changed man; he was no longer content with a life of wealth and the frivolities of society. In 1919 he retired to Paris to help run the American Hospital there. Before the couple divorced, Marjorie, a statuesque apple-cheeked redhead, started receiving "armloads of roses" from a dynamic businessman whose mushrooming brokerage company had earned him a

fortune that rivaled J. P. Morgan's, according to the authors of *Palm Beach Babylon.*

Marjorie married E. F. Hutton in 1920. Her only child with Edward Francis Hutton became the movie star Dina Merrill. Meanwhile, Marjorie's new brother-in-law, Franklyn Hutton, married another of the nation's wealthiest young women, Edna Woolworth, the daughter of the dime-store founder. Their daughter became the famous Barbara Hutton, who married six times but was seldom happy and who squandered her legendary fortune on endless extravagant travel and some of her freeloading husbands.

The Roaring Twenties were the most excessive time for moneyed fun seekers, and Palm Beach became the ultimate place for the energetic expression of what money could buy and maintain. According to Eliot Kleinberg, author of *Wicked Palm Beach*, "In Palm Beach, as elsewhere in South Florida, prohibition barely put a dent in the partying. During the Prohibition Era the Royal Poinciana Hotel . . . featured a secret hallway that led to a clandestine speakeasy called 'Hypocrite's Row.' From rum-runners to pirates, mobsters to moguls, Palm Beach County has hosted its fair share of questionable characters." Also around this time, some ragtag bands of violent criminals like the infamous Ashley Gang had much of South Florida's population gripped in fear.

During the outrageously hedonistic period between World War I and the Great Depression, in Palm Beach it was Marjorie and E. F. Hutton who epitomized the idealized power couple whose colossal fortunes, whirlwind socializing, and happy-go-lucky enjoyment of their fineries fascinated everyone and helped to turn the island into one big nonstop party.

Despite Prohibition, the world's finest liquor arrived regularly at the island's docks. Showman Florenz Ziegfeld helped hostesses like Marjorie mount shimmering costume balls at which popular entertainers such as Al Jolson performed. As early as

1925, the George Gershwin musical *Tip Toes* used Palm Beach as its setting. When Gershwin's friend, New York moneyman Emil Mosbacher, rented a home in Palm Beach on South Ocean Boulevard with his wife and his three children, Gershwin came down to stay with the family and spent the winter of 1933 writing variations of his song "I've Got Rhythm."

In the mid-1920s, the Huttons started to expand the Postum Cereal Company that Marjorie had inherited into a giant conglomerate called General Foods by acquiring and incorporating such brands as Jell-O, Birds Eye frozen foods, Log Cabin syrup, and many more. By this time there were several high-wrought mansions in Palm Beach similar in size to Mizner's El Mirasol. These showy new Palm Beach estates belonged to the likes of Pittsburgh Coal Company chairman William G. Warren; tobacco heiress Mary Duke and her husband, Anthony Biddle Jr. of Philadelphia; and Wall Street brokerage head Edward Shearson. Soon Mizner had two major architect competitors, Maurice Fatio and Marion Sims Wyeth, and all of them quickly transformed the scrub of the island.

Marjorie turned to Wyeth with the explicit intention of wanting to build a palace to outdo Eva Stotesbury's El Mirasol. Wyeth in turn hired Joseph Urban, famous for his elaborate Metropolitan Opera sets, to design the interiors. In 1927, the Huttons' Mar-a-Lago, meaning "sea to lake," was completed on 17.7 acres. The dazzling and unique tropical palazzo, with towers and flourishes inspired by European castles and *Arabian Nights* tales, had 115 rooms.

The two-story Venetian-style living room was breathtakingly ornamented with frescoes and custom-made chandeliers. Its forty-two bedrooms were all furnished in different styles, including French, English, Portuguese, and Old Dutch. The complex structure, famous for its intricately laid out, balconied, and columned patio, was surrounded by a citrus grove and a

nine-hole golf course. A private tunnel under South Ocean Boulevard led to the family's 450-foot private beach and to a back entry to Palm Beach's exclusive Bath & Tennis Club.

Mar-a-Lago was the scene of spectacular costume balls, recitals, supper dances, teas, charity benefits, and even Broadway show performances. When the Huttons needed a rest from all the partying, they would sail off to some faraway place like Tahiti on their yacht, *Hussar V*, considered at the time the world's most sumptuously outfitted private boat, which had a crew of seventy-two.

E. F.'s infidelities and Marjorie's exuberant spending contributed to the destruction of the fifteen-year marriage. After the divorce, he transferred the title of the *Hussar V* to Marjorie and resigned as chairman of the General Foods Corporation. She renamed the yacht *Sea Cloud* and then married an influential Washington lawyer and lobbyist named Joseph Davies, who became U.S. ambassador to the Soviet Union in 1937.

The couple was featured on the cover of *Time* magazine just before sailing off on Marjorie's five-million-dollar *Sea Cloud* to the communist country. Once in Moscow, the couple entertained many exalted figures of the day—including Charles Lindbergh, history-making European and Asian diplomats, and various royals—and sailed the waters of Finland, Sweden, Germany, and Poland.

Ambassador Davies, however, was insensitive to the obvious challenges of a relationship between the democratic United States and the totalitarian Soviet Union during Stalin's purges. In January 1938, Davies was transferred to Brussels as ambassador to Belgium. His diplomatic and political role started to fade after the war years, and he became abusive toward Marjorie. She divorced him, swearing never to marry again.

But in 1958 at the age of seventy-one she married for the fourth time, a Westinghouse executive from Pittsburgh named Herbert May. They both loved square dancing and started to hold country music hoedowns at Mar-a-Lago every Thursday. There, judges,

doctors, and other professionals—quite a different group from the usual Palm Beach partygoers—would come together. Formal dinners for visitors like the Maharaja of Baroda, Saudi princes, and the Duke and Duchess of Windsor always included something from General Foods, including desserts made with Jell-O.

At age eighty-one, by which time Marjorie had legally taken back the name Post, she almost married again, a former secretary of the navy twenty years her junior. However, her children and her grandchildren managed to dissuade her.

Among Marjorie and her daughters, the Post cereal heiresses, there was a total of sixteen marriages. The Close sisters, Adelaide and Eleanor, accounted for three and six marriages, respectively; Eleanor's first husband was the still struggling, talented future movie giant Preston Sturges, and Dina Merrill had three husbands, among them the actor Cliff Robertson.

Lilly Pulitzer was quite a breed apart from Marjorie Merriweather Post; nevertheless, the relentless partying and resultant drama of Palm Beach would in time also affect the Pulitzer marriage. If Peter chafed at his consort role to Lilly's standing as the resort's presumptive reigning royal, the struggle did not show, but behind the chiseled features and appealing air of confidence, Peter was a complex man. Having been deprived of a mother's love since boyhood, lacking the clubby proclivity of other Palm Beach scions, and, in a money-conscious town, having inherited a lot less than was generally assumed, he had developed a protective, defensive shell.

With Lilly's growing national celebrity status and admiration coming in from everywhere, though, for a while it was a heady time for both Lilly and Peter.

"They were terrific together," recalled bandleader Peter Duchin, a friend of the couple, to Laura Jacobs in *Vanity Fair*.

"They were very close. . . . He was racy. I mean in the sense of just jumping into his plane and flying off . . . into his orange groves and work in the fields with the Seminole people."

To most people who met Peter for the first time, he came across as a he-man, a sportsman, his own man. He liked to talk about his off-the-beaten-track fishing adventures, the chores he tended to on his cattle ranch, and his latest hotel ventures in Miami. Lilly and Peter were visibly affectionate with each other and with their children, Peter Jr., Minnie, and Liza.

Recalling her childhood in the same *Vanity Fair* article, Minnie Pulitzer McCluskey mused, "You never saw such hugging and kissing. Everyone wanted to be them." In the mid-1960s Lilly and Peter were singled out for their buoyant individualism and exuberant lifestyle by three influential observers of the changing society landscape in three books: *The Fashionable Savages* by John Fairchild, *The Beautiful People* by Marylin Bender, and *The World of Fashion* by Eleanor Lambert, inventor of the best-dressed list. Lilly had the world at her bare feet.

"Lilly Pulitzer was America's Pucci," recalled fashion historian June Weir over tea and watercress sandwiches at New York's Four Seasons Hotel. At the time Lilly launched her fashion business Weir was top editor of *Women's Wear Daily*, soon after which John Fairchild named her head fashion editor of *W* magazine. "Just as Pucci shocked the eye with color, she was one of the first Americans to understand the importance of colorful prints. Up until that time prints were dowdy. She did them in a young way. She did them with such fun and such joy that it really made you want to wear prints. She, like Pucci, bridged that period of moving from the more sedate Fifties to the youth-quake of the Sixties. His were more geometric, abstract, graphic, sophisticated optical illusion motifs, color and form in fuschia and geranium, lavender and banana, tortoise shell and cardinal red, hundreds of hues dissected, recomposed, reinvented. She was more fun. Lilly's

prints and colors talked to you. You saw pictures. They made you feel good. Even today, there is something refreshing about them. Her clothes were feminine. While they were minimal, they came out looking very feminine."

At the same time that ebullient photographs of Lilly and her husband were cropping up in glossies everywhere, with the unique Pulitzer prints cleverly unfurled around them on tabletops, tossed on sofas, in the shape of huge pillows or shown off in the clothing worn by their good-looking friends and their children, an increasing emotional distance was developing between Peter and Lilly. "Actually, work was drawing both Peter and Lilly further into their own lives," concluded Laura Jacobs in her July 2003 *Vanity Fair* article. She quoted a fashion column by Eugenia Sheppard in which Sheppard stated that the husbands of Lilly and her early business partner, Laura, hardly ever saw their busy wives "except to say good night and good morning." Then Jacobs quoted Lilly saying, "Peter and I couldn't wait to get out the door. Let's see who can work the longest, the hardest." Several of their friends, however, believe that those long hours apart may have actually prolonged the marriage.

Palm Beach is the zenith of tropical American playgrounds. As such it is not an ideal place for a troubled union.

With his drop-dead good looks recognized by all the media, Peter was part of Lilly's public image, and in that role he enhanced her fashion label, but this also meant more exposure for him than he had been used to. Did any of it go to his head? He was much more than a decorative foil for her admired style and her continually imaginative products. Did he occasionally feel the need to assert his own undeniable appeal, especially to the opposite sex? What about Lilly's Sneaky Pete men's nightshirts—perhaps the name implied something about her husband?

Lilly was a well-bred young woman who never complained, never explained, and never showed sadness; taciturn Scorpio that she was, she held back whatever bothered her, so she never elaborated on any sneaky Pete problem, if she suspected or knew that there was one. Not a word was said to even her closest friends.

But a striking brunette Frenchwoman living in New York and married to an American who for years was close to Peter's sister, Patsy, recalls meeting Peter at the time during her first visit to Palm Beach. "He was incredibly good-looking and full of personal charm. He oozed with charm. Oo la la," she said, swooning. "And when he spoke with you he would turn that charm on full blast, occasionally putting his arms around your shoulders as if to half hug you or embrace you. He would completely concentrate on you as if you were the only woman in the room or as if he had been waiting all his life to meet you and talk to you. He was irresistible. Without question the sexiest guy in Palm Beach."

There were rumors, she recalls, of Peter's blatant flirtations, which shocked some of the locals. When one friend reprimanded him about having his arm around a pretty woman's waist during most of a cocktail party, Peter shrugged, "It's my life." Some people swore that Peter had become a tricky womanizer. There were whispers that he would buy transatlantic airline tickets for women he fancied and promise to meet them in Paris. Word got around in the small town that sometimes he'd turn up overseas, but frequently the young woman would be stranded alone in Europe because Peter was a no-show.

As a seaside holiday pleasure center, Palm Beach never lacked its seasonal influx of fresh feminine beauties, but in the 1960s the more conservative old-line American enclave experienced an intrusion of jet-set flamboyance. In a tropical-heat setting

there is always more show of skin, more body exposure, more temptation, and a constant redefinition of social attitudes about what constitutes modesty and the limits of seductive behavior. Among the resort's wealthy and attractive scions of family fortunes, forbidden liaisons unburdened by the usual emotional markers were never uncommon. And, of course, the late 1960s saw the emergence of the sexual revolution, with plenty of entitled characters ready and eager to push the conventional moral boundaries.

Also in the 1960s, the bikini made its entry on U.S. seashores. Beautiful aquatic women have been recurring fantasy figures since ancient times, when sirens, mermaids, and water nymphs led mythology heroes astray. Beach resorts all across the country started staging beauty pageants as early as the 1920s, associating feminine beauty with one-piece bathing suits and high heels in the male imagination.

Soon after the bikini appeared in the United States, *Sports Illustrated* debuted its annual swimsuit issue in 1964, probably the most relevant modern incarnation of the bathing beauty. Showing active, healthy-looking, athletic-looking women, *Sports Illustrated* reflected the changing cultural attitudes and sexual standards.

With all of the water sports—bodysurfing, sailing, waterskiing, fishing, and yachting—along with constant poolside parties and swimming, the bikini made a major splash in Palm Beach. A series of well-toned curvy Palm Beach women like Susan Hutton, Camilla Hoover, Agneta Hitchcock, and Lil Kinsolving appeared in the pages and on covers of *Town & Country* magazine in the late 1960s and early 1970s.

Palm Beach is perennially regenerating itself. New tycoons and new divorcées regularly arrive in town seeking love and adventure. In the 1960s, Lilly Pulitzer was responsible for a reassessment and

recharging of the town. Her earthy type of beauty, her business empire, and her social preeminence made it smarter to work than to just play. Other Palm Beach women imitated her by opening shops all over town.

Once the richest heiress in Cuba, Julia Aspuru Rousseau opened a boutique near Lilly's in the Via Mizner called Salon Français with two other Cuban exiles, Lourdes Rich and Bibi Santeiro. Soon after that, a colorfully embroidered Mexican version of the beach chemise designed by Nelly Wulff of Puerto Vallarta appeared in a shop called La Palapa in Royal Poinciana Plaza, which was opened by Judy Krampf.

Elizabeth "Betty" Stettinus Trippe, wife of high-profile Pan American Airlines chairman Juan Trippe, launched an exciting gift boutique on Peruvian Avenue a few months later. Even Lilly's mother, Lillian Phipps, Palm Beach hostess supreme in her fabulous Moresque villa, caught the fever and established a Palm Beach art gallery.

The decades between Lilly's era and Marjorie Merriweather Post's era (1922 to 1962) are considered the resort's halcyon days, when the likes of Walter Chrysler, Willis du Pont, and Henry Ford II rubbed shoulders with Clark Gable, Cary Grant, and Douglas Fairbanks Jr. while enchanting and pursuing the island's many beautiful, well-born, or socially ambitious women.

Art collector Jayne Wrightsman, in her Louis XV–furnished French antique-filled villa; cosmetics businesswoman Estée Lauder, with footmen behind every guest at her dining table; and the irrepressible and witty jewelry designer Dysie Davie, alluringly starring in her many strapless gowns; all threw sumptuous parties for visitors like Winston Churchill; Loel and Gloria Guinness (of the Guinness brewing and banking family); Rosalind Russell and her Broadway-producer husband, Fred Bresson; actress Beatrice Lillie,

who had become Lady Peel; Bing Crosby; Joan Crawford; the Marquess of Blandford, who would soon inherit the title Duke of Marlborough; and the Duke and Duchess of Windsor.

During these glamorous years, every new high season in Palm Beach ushered in yet one more glittering ball devoted to raising big money for yet another important charity. The phenomenon was inspired by the success of the annual Heart Ball, held on Valentine's Day, which brought down a battalion of foreign diplomats from Washington, D.C. Every ambassador arrived decked out in full regalia, complete with glistening epaulets and tons of shiny decorations. Within a few years, resort regulars found themselves supporting a nonstop merry-go-round of black-tie and white-tie-and-tails events devoted to advance medical research. By the sixties there was a ball to fight virtually every human ailment and benefit every organ in the body.

Although she generously subscribed to all these causes and usually attended the galas in one of her famous diamond tiaras, Marjorie Merriweather Post, by the late fifties, was viewed more like the resort's dowager empress. There was now yet another Queen of Palm Beach in place. Her name was Mary Sanford, and she spearheaded virtually every charity committee in town, The wife of wealthy polo player Stephen "Laddie" Sanford, heir to the lucrative Bigelow-Sanford carpet mills of upstate New York, she had appeared as Mary Duncan in sixteen Hollywood films directed by the likes of Murnau and Borzage. But it was not until after she was introduced by Marion Davies and William Randolph Hearst to Sanford and her arrival in Palm Beach in 1933 that her fun-loving, sexy, hard-charging person-ality established her as a real-life star. In her oceanfront villa, Los Incas, notable for its mosaic walls made entirely of sea-shells, she turned her energies to charity work. She represented a changing, more social-conscious partying elite. Of course, there was the incentive of tax write-offs. Nevertheless, young

Palm Beach matrons vied with one another to get their names on Mary's ball committee lists.

Lilly's and Peter Pulitzer's names only infrequently made the Shiny Sheet's report on who was at which benefit the night before. Because of the multitude of demands on their time by their expanding businesses and their clear preference for barefoot relaxation with their children versus top hats and tiaras, they were two young denizens of the community going about their lives in sharp contrast to this older, more frenzied social scene.

CHAPTER 10

Lilly's New Love

ALTHOUGH EVEN EUROPEAN ROYALS AND FAMOUS U.S. tycoons like Henry Ford II and Estée Lauder had their occasional awkward moments trying to insert themselves into the Palm Beach social swim, over the years two sets of foreigners, the Canadians and the Cubans, seem to have been exceptionally good at getting the hang of the golden resort's unique mix of formality and playfulness, elegance and ease. On the whole, these two groups seem to have had no trouble leaping gracefully into the island's coveted private-party circuit and exclusive club scene.

The Canadians were made up of families accustomed to escaping their frozen northlands every winter and genuinely relished the warm-weather sports of island life in such former British colonial outposts as Bermuda, the Bahamas, and the British West Indies. They had already acquired a taste for the slowed-down, lightened-up rhythm of the

tropics, where certain expectations of dress and rules of civilized congeniality nevertheless required their acquiescence.

Some of the affluent heads of families from the cities of Montreal, Toronto, and Winnipeg as well as from the Maritime Provinces had been schooled partly in Britain and were skilled at the witty repartee admired by the Anglophile American power elite. In contrast to certain newcomers from places like Alabama or Texas, who were eager to flaunt their shiny new accoutrements of wealth, the Canadians tended to practice restraint. Above all, they understood the fine points of clubsmanship and the tribal quality of American upper-class culture.

The Cubans arrived in Palm Beach in 1960, most of them dispossessed after Castro's revolution did away with the props of privilege. They were among the seven hundred thousand Cubans, mostly from the country's middle and upper classes, who flooded into Florida from Havana, a city ninety miles away from Key West.

Many of them fled after losing everything and were willing to work in any menial job to provide for their families. Others came with sterling social connections, educations acquired at top American universities, and sizable bank accounts in the United States and Europe. But they arrived from a distinctly different culture, and being Spanish-speaking, they had to rise above parochial perceptions and hostilities they encountered. They tried to make their way in their new situation of exile and find a means by which to restore their family fortunes and replicate their once sophisticated lifestyles.

The Cuban families who took refuge in Palm Beach—including the Aguileras, the Aspurus, the Azquetas, the Fanjuls, and the Rousseaus—were wealthy from the sugar business. They had owned vast tracts of land all over the island, had planted sugarcane for generations, owned substantial numbers of highly profitable sugar mills, and built palatial houses.

Their homes typically had grand entrances flanked by Corinthian columns, with extraordinary rooms boasting coffered ceilings, intricate wood paneling, floors of Italian marble, and white marble staircases with splendid wrought-iron railings. Many of these Cubans were descendants of Spanish aristocrats as well as of the Cuban national heroes who won independence from Spain in 1898 after thirty years of fighting.

Elegiac tales have been told of Cuba's pre-Castro days, and stories of the excesses that justify revolutions have also been passed down and often exaggerated.

An example is the occasion on which the richest of the rich sugar kings of Cuba, Julio Lobo, supposedly filled his swimming pool with perfume so the visiting MGM star Esther Williams could have an unforgettable time practicing her laps. Lobo's island estate, Tinguaro, was his legendary Shangri-la, to which he used to invite writers, artists, diplomats, and such luminaries as Ginger Rogers, Maurice Chevalier, Richard Burton, Merle Oberon, and cartoonist Charles Addams.

One tall, dapper young man, whose command of English was exceptional and whose verbal cleverness and unconventional sense of humor would unfailingly enliven any gathering, was frequently at these soirees. His name was Enrique Rousseau. A high-spirited lawyer from a patrician Cuban family, Enrique had gone to Johns Hopkins University for his undergraduate studies but had returned to Cuba to receive his law degree from the University of Havana.

Enrique seemed to be everywhere in those days. Accompanied by his brother Pepito, he made the rounds of Havana's fabled nightclubs, where the conga lines and rumba rhythms never stopped and their boozy pal Errol Flynn never wanted to call it a night. One day, Enrique was unexpectedly called to rush to his friend Ernest Hemingway's Finca Vigia on the outskirts of Havana to perform a special favor. Sure enough, Enrique Rousseau's name pops up in old newspaper clippings as the young notary

who officiated at the second wedding of Winston Guest to a stylish standout blonde from Boston named Lucy Cochrane, who would soon become the fashion icon and queen of American high society C. Z. Guest.

Descended from French planters who had left nearby Haiti during one of the many bloody conflicts in that island's turbulent history, Enrique's forebears settled on Cuba's southeastern tip between Guantanamo Bay and the Sierra Maestra mountains to start another sugar plantation. Enrique was very international; he visited Madrid, Paris, and London and went on a safari in what was called East Africa with Hemingway in the early 1950s. Wherever he went, especially on his visits in Hollywood with Richard Burton, he always had great stories to tell on his return.

"Enrique was tall, handsome, with manners and charm; but if there is one word that best describes him, it's . . . *fun*," recalls Gonzalo Garcia-Pedroso, who now lives in Miami but was a teenage boy in Havana when he met Rousseau. The only son of older parents, Garcia-Pedroso was inadvertently drawn into the juicy gossip of adults, a sport beloved by Cuban society then and now. He remembers all of his mother's friends chattering away about Enrique's playboy exploits and his undeniable sex appeal. They often wondered who would be the lucky girl who would catch Enrique, because, these adults always added, "underneath the fun he is very smart and a true gentleman."

The lucky girl was Julia Aspuru. Elegant, dark-haired, warm, and refined, Julia was one of three very popular daughters of the second richest sugar king in Havana, Manuel Aspuru. He had inherited the thriving Toledo sugar mill from his family and wanted to hire Lobo before he became a competitor. Aspuru often traveled to the United States. He represented Cuba's sugar growers' interests whenever the mechanics of shipping, U.S. quotas, and the economics of the industry warranted complicated negotiations with Cuba's giant neighbor to the north, its main market.

Running a sugar plantation was a most uneven occupation. Things would get madly busy when the sugarcane was being cut. The rest of the year on a plantation could be idle and isolating, because unlike other agricultural products, sugar grows by itself. In 1911, a newsletter circulated by the American Cane Growers' Association reported on "the organization of a new company called The Central Cuba Sugar Company when Sr. Jose Rousseau has bought out his partners in the ownership of Central Union in Santiago de Cuba, thus becoming sole owner of the mill."

Enrique's family's would have liked its property to benefit from Enrique's managerial authority to sign off on deals, but unlike the sons of most sugar men, the newly married lawyer accepted a prestigious offer to head Cuba's Tobacco Institute and live in Havana with his fashionable wife, Julia. A few years later, the couple became the parents of two girls, Sandra and Toinette.

In 1960, when Enrique and Julia left Cuba with their children, they set out for Florida by boat. They were able to load most of their prized French antique furniture on the vessel, along with some favorite art objects. Also leaving their homeland with them was Julia's sister Bibi and her husband, Manuel Santeiro, Enrique's closest friend; Julia's other sister, Lourdes; and their parents, Manuel Aspuru and his wife, Maria Antonia Alonso.

Because they had good memories of visiting friends in Palm Beach, and because of their longtime acquaintance with the former U.S. ambassador to Cuba, Earl E. T. Smith, who was later mayor of Palm Beach, the new immigrants decided to settle in the resort rather than in Miami, where 65 percent of their exiled friends were headed. Garcia-Pedroso remembers how tender and supportive these families were to one another.

"Just tell me what you want, not what you need," former sugar baron Jose (Pepe) Gomez Mena would tell people in those early months, then he would write out a check, according to Garcia-Pedroso. The man who once made world news with an al fresco dinner he gave shortly after the war in honor of King Leopold III of Belgium by ringing flower-wreathed banquettes around the pool of his Country Club Park mansion in the most exclusive neighborhood in Havana wanted his proud but now poor friends to feel that instead of a charity handout they were doing business with him.

The newly migrated Cubans banded together to build a street in Palm Beach, which they named Kawama Lane after the exclusive hotel on Cuba's Veradero Beach. The immigrant families included the sugar-rich Fanjul and Gomez Mena families and the Aguileras, wealthy descendants of fighters against Spanish rule who owned cattle ranches and rice and sugar plantations. The Aguileras had a son, Guillermo, and two daughters, Alina and Elena, who, in the words of a Miami friend, had everything: brains, beauty, and breeding.

The February 1950 issue of *Life* magazine gave its readers a glimpse into the stylish private realm of Cuba's top families in an article titled "The Cuba That American Rum and Rumba Tourists Never Saw." The piece featured the Gomez Menas' annual Christmas party, held in their exquisite white tower-topped mansion built in 1913 by the second president of Cuba, Jose Miguel Gomez , today the Museum of Decorative Arts. Photographs taken on its picturesque rooftop loggia that commanded a sweeping view of the city depicted a dozen Havana women wearing their latest couture gowns purchased in Paris or from Christian Dior himself on one of the rare trips he made across the Atlantic.

Dior would make stops only in Havana and New York. His arrival in Havana—rather than Buenos Aires, Rio de Janeiro, or Mexico City—was a signal to the world of what an exciting pulse

point Havana had become for all that was trendy, new, and culturally sophisticated in those spirited postwar years. Indeed, Dior's visit elicited oohs and aahs from the chic upper-crust women from all of the Latin American countries who would descend en masse on the Cuban capital for the treat of seeing the master couturier's creations firsthand.

Another *Life* magazine article chronicled in photographs a day in the life of "Havana glamour girl" Alina Johnson Aguilera. Until this coverage, Cubans may have been perceived in the United States as exotic, but this showed their discernment about the clothes they wore and the schools their children attended as well as how well versed they were in American culture, the result of fifty years of geographic proximity and direct exposure to modern U.S. advances and accoutrements.

The Aspurus, the Santeiros, and the Rousseaus were more influenced by Europe and had more of a Francophile bent in their tastes than the Aguileras, the Fanjuls, or the Gomez Menas, some of whom had one American grandparent or whose children had married Americans, but they made a Herculean effort to acclimate themselves to their new base. To help cover the private school tuitions of their daughters, who were attending the Sacred Heart Academy in Manhattan and Foxcroft in Virginia, Julia Rousseau and her sister Bibi Santeiro opened a fashion boutique called Salon Français on Via Mizner, directly across from Lilly Pulitzer's boutique. It was quite a novelty, featuring French ready-to-wear and custom-made items, and it was a hit.

Working across the street from each other, Julia and Lilly became friends. They had much in common: not only their shops and their interest in selling clothes but also their love of their families, their fondness for animals, and their passion for gardening. Julia was a connoisseur of roses, Lilly of tropical blooms. Both were

generous and inspired hostesses. Meanwhile, their husbands, Enrique and Peter, also forged a friendship.

Some years after the Rousseaus settled in Palm Beach, they gave a party that was the talk of the resort. Among their guests were the infamous Dominican playboy Porfirio Rubirosa, Zsa Zsa Gabor, and Kim Novak. Social columns of the mid-1960s are full of items mentioning the Rousseaus, the Santeiros, and the Pulitzers dining together at Nando's, having drinks together at Taboo, and, contrary to Lilly's protestations in media interviews that she eschewed Palm Beach galas, attending several charity balls together. The three couples clearly enjoyed one another's company; they all loved to dance, felt comfortable together, and shared occasional secrets after a few drinks, as close friends are wont to do.

The third and perhaps the most gregarious and enterprising of the Aspuru girls, Lourdes, moved to Madrid, where she opened the famous jet-set discotheque Topaz and married a successful Spanish businessman, Carlos Musso.

The Fanjuls were able to recover from the enormous loss of their sugarcane mills, refineries, distilleries, and significant amounts of real estate in Cuba. They started over by buying four thousand acres of land near Lake Okeechobee and some sugar mills in Louisiana.

In time, the Fanjul Corporation came to own 155,000 acres in Palm Beach County; today it owns and operates the umbrella company Florida Crystals Inc. In addition to its vast land holdings in Florida, Florida Crystals lays claim to 240,000 acres in the Dominican Republic, where the family built the luxury resort hotel Casa de Campo in 1986. Florida Crystals is now the principal sugar producer in the United States and sells several major brands, such as Domino Sugar and Flo-Sun Sugar.

While Emilia and Pepe Fanjul's children were growing up, Emilia made it her business to participate in Palm Beach community affairs; she was active in the PTA at the Palm Beach Day Academy,

where by the year 2012, twenty-three members of the Fanjul family had been educated. She began to take a major role in planning special events like casual barbecues for young families with children at the aging but still coveted Bath & Tennis Club. This endeared her and her husband to many of the offspring of the club's ruling old guard. Today the two are close friends of the king of Spain and of Senator Marco Rubio. The Fanjuls are at the apex of the Palm Beach social pyramid, right up there with the Canadians, Hilary and Galen Weston, billionaires who are friends of Queen Elizabeth and Prince Philip.

Enrique, by contrast, had a harder time with his sugar ventures in the United States. When he encountered problems with his Central Florida sugar mill and engaged in a series of bitter legal fights—all of which he won—the couple's marriage started cracking. They divorced, then almost as soon as they received their papers they remarried. Not long after their second wedding, Enrique and Julia quietly separated again but did not file for a second divorce until after their daughter's wedding to a Houstonite two years later, in 1969. Enrique went to work with Peter Pulitzer, who was branching out into hotels in Miami and needed someone to supervise the building of his latest project, the Howard Johnson Hotel there. Peter asked Enrique to manage the new hotel. During this time, Enrique—single again and now spending half of his time in Miami—stayed with Peter and Lilly when he was in Palm Beach.

Meanwhile Peter was traveling a lot, flying back and forth to Europe. He was intent on expanding his hotel holdings abroad and was working on a deal with KLM to develop tourist hotels in Indonesia, spending extensive time in negotiations in the Netherlands.

When Peter was a child he had acquired a taste for long jaunts and living the good life in the best hotels of Rome, Paris, and London through his father, who had pursued the most beautiful

women he could find wherever they were. Little wonder that the example rubbed off on the son, who like his father was an agile conversationalist and liked being the center of attention. In most people's minds Peter had enjoyed his premarriage reputation as the most eligible bachelor of Palm Beach and being seen with the likes of Grace Kelly and Jackie Bouvier in public, though they believe that he was never in love with any girl until he met and married Lilly. Back in those days *Palm Beach Life* magazine wrote about him, "Peter is one of the new breed of playboys with the significant difference that work is their play. They live well but quietly. Stimulation comes primarily from discovering the new and challenging." Now, nearing forty and financially secure, the restlessness and love of the chase that had been part of his personality came back with a vengeance. His need for conquests increasingly intruded on his commitment to marriage and family life.

It did not help that Peter's best friend in Palm Beach at this time was the consummate playboy, sportsman, and "swashbuckler," as he liked to refer to himself, Jim Kimberly, who according to the authors of *Palm Beach Babylon*, Murray Weiss and Bill Hoffmann, "considered his adventurous nature his life's work." As one of the heirs to the huge Kimberly Clark Kleenex tissue fortune, he had a well-known inheritance of fifty million dollars and for a couple of decades nearly owned Palm Beach. Kimberly's family in Neenah, Wisconsin, had groomed him to become a leader of the family business. But like Peter Pulitzer, Kimberly was a college dropout. He used to boast that his resumé consisted of the following occupations: race-car driver, yachtsman, sport fisherman, big game hunter, world-class traveler, and romancer of the world's most beautiful women. Kimberly was in his fifties and twice divorced when he bought a Palm Beach villa near the Pulitzers on Lake Worth, not far from the Sailfish Club, where Peter liked to hang out.

It is hard to imagine that in the small, gossipy resort town, which had direct pipelines to every international capital, the skirt-chasing exploits of these much-traveling, sporting and striking-looking buddies did not reach Lilly's ears or those of her friends'. Still, when news of the dissolution of the Pulitzer marriage came into the open, friends, family, the media—everyone—seemed to express surprise and shock. The reaction was not unlike the one that had greeted the news years before when people first heard that Peter Pulitzer and Lilly McKim had eloped.

Like most men who feel entitled to play around but when the safe and comfortable home life they've been accustomed to is pulled out from under them, Peter, by all accounts, was very upset.

Years later, when a friend of both Lilly's and Peter's, Kirk Henckels, was going through a Palm Beach divorce, he remembers Peter coming across a crowded party to put an arm consolingly on his shoulder: " Listen buddy, I know just how you feel," he sympathized. "It's a pretty rotten thing to have happen. I know just what you're going through. I was just about your age when Lilly and I split. Forty with no idea what to do or where to go next."

Peter had deep family roots in the town, so some sympathy was on his side. At Peter's suggestion, Enrique had moved into Peter and Lilly's house when he was in Palm Beach, and Enrique, relatively new in the community and a foreigner to boot, bore the brunt of the nasty talk going around: "Not only did he move into Pulitzer's house but he moved in on Pulitzer's wife." These rumors were assiduously countered by Lilly's many friends and members of the community. By this time they had come to like Enrique very much and considered him a proper gentleman, in the full sense of the word.

No one knows exactly what happened next, mainly because of Lilly's secret-keeping nature. Conjecture is that through the years of Peter's philandering the chasm that had developed between

him and Lilly could no longer be bridged. And Enrique and Lilly, who had known each other as trusted friends for years, fell in love. When Peter returned from one of his overseas trips, Lilly informed him that she was filing for a divorce. The Pulitzers reached a quiet out-of-court settlement and Lilly maintained custody of their children. Years later Liza Pulitzer admitted that the divorce was hard on the children because they never witnessed a fight between their parents; none of them saw it coming.

A few days after her divorce from Peter became final, Lilly and Enrique got married, on November 27, 1969, Thanksgiving weekend. The wedding was held in Lilly's house with just their immediate families present. Afterward Lillian and Ogden Phipps celebrated their daughter's union with a formal sit-down dinner—just for family members—at their home.

The following January the Rousseaus flew to England and Italy on a six-week European honeymoon.

Vanity Fair quoted Lilly once describing Enrique to a Palm Beach friend named Nancy Kezele as "The handsomest person I've ever seen in my life."

"She was so much in love, I've never seen anything like it," recalled one of Lillian Phipps's friends, Caroline Hudson Firestone, one night over dinner. "With whom?" Two of the dinner guests asked simultaneously. "Enrique, of course. I remember sitting next to her being in the middle of conversation, when she spotted him coming up the boardwalk. Her face, her whole being seemed transformed. She seemed to tremble, her eyes were ablaze, she then totally melted, with a facial expression as if she were in another world, Once he was near, they fell into each other's arms." Firestone went on to say that Enrique gave her "something she never had before."

Most people agree with Lilly's friend Peter Duchin's assessment of what attracted Lilly to Enrique: "He had a great sense of calm about him. I think Lilly confided in him a lot, which she

doesn't do with many people. He made her feel protected. He was humorous, he was attractive, and he was very solid."

Lilly and Enrique shared the same serendipitous sense of fun and grasp of life's fundamentals. Enrique's easygoing, tolerant, buoyant personality and lawyerly intelligence were good for Lilly, and she in turn was supportive of him. Lilly embraced the customs, irresistible music, and spicy-sweet cooking of his Cuban heritage. After a night of square dancing at Marjorie Merriweather Post's Mar-a-Lago, to which Enrique wore a traditional Cuban peasant shirt, Lilly decided to add to her men's fashion line a version of the tailored overshirt in a dizzying array of her preppy tropical prints as a suggested jacket alternative for hot evenings. The Lilly *guayabera* was a great success.

Two lovable people had found each other and a lasting love. The marriage turned out to be a very happy one.

Four years later, in one of those twists of fate that give Palm Beach its incestuous reputation, Enrique's ex-wife, Julia Rousseau, married Peter Pulitzer's half-brother Charles Amory Jr. And yes, after the initial dust settled, with time all parties remained on speaking terms.

CHAPTER 11

The Stormy Season

I N THE 1980S ·AND THE 1990S, SEVERAL MISFORTUNES converged to darken Lilly's golden life. While her marriage to Enrique continued to bring her bliss, in 1982 she was forced to deal with two highly unpleasant and deeply unsettling occurrences from the outside world almost simultaneously. Then there were serious health problems to deal with.

By the early 1980s Lilly's firm, of which she had been the sole owner and designer for more than twenty years, had sashayed merrily through the 1960s and 1970s, capturing devotees across the country through thirty-one stores in some of the wealthiest places in the United States. It was a wonderful position for a fashion firm to be in. Her company's sales in 1982 were fifteen million dollars.

Still, in the fickle fashion industry, cycles come and go. Suddenly the winds of change came riffling through the nation's design ateliers, and it was no longer such a happy

time for a dress like the Lilly. Typical of the times was that Grace Mirabella, a more sedate, sensible, and practical-minded editor in chief, had taken over as the high priestess of fashion at *Vogue* magazine from the flamboyant, colorful, and idiosyncratic Diana Vreeland. At this powerful post, which influenced both designers and buyers, it was now Mirabella who decreed what was in and what was out.

The 1980s were a new era of power suits and dressing for success, with padded-shouldered jackets, cinched-in waists, and low-voltage fabrics in black, gray, and beige. Bright colors were out. Neutral tones and murky earth hues were in. Women in the workforce favored tailored monochromatic pantsuits by Giorgio Armani, Calvin Klein, and Donna Karan. Dress for success was a phrase that these women took seriously. Women with boardroom ambitions wanted to blend in with their male counterparts in pinstriped suits. Innocent childlike-shaped dresses in joyous crayon colors did not fit the eighties zeitgeist, and delight in leisure—Lilly's specialty—seemed beside the point.

In 1983 Lilly tried to join the spirit of the times by catering to the increasing number of working women with a new division of easy-to-move-in, work-in separates in toned-down colors and comfortable fabrics. She called this line New Directions. But it turned out to be the wrong direction. To remedy the situation, she brought in a new management team and cut back the number of her boutiques from thirty-one to twenty-six. "It was a very unstructured company," she told *California Apparel News*. "A lot of people did their own thing. I wouldn't say the firm suffered for it, but it could have had we allowed things to continue as they were. I'm never going to be business-oriented, but the company nevertheless has had an about face."

This did not happen, though; there was no turnaround. As popular as Lilly's clothing had been, even just two years before this, her business folded in 1984—or in Lilly's inimitable words,

"It croaked." By the end of 1984, the firm was in bankruptcy. She told Larissa MacFarquhar of the *New Yorker* somewhat irritatedly, "After 25 years, it was done, for God's sake!" Before she filed for bankruptcy, she paid every bill at all of her boutiques across the country, many of which were run by personal friends who needed jobs.

"I started it as a lark and I followed my whim," she explained to Lorna Koski in a *Sun Sentinel* interview. Lilly was convinced that her company had folded because she "didn't know enough to keep up with the times." But one of her Palm Beach friends thought that Lilly was getting a little tired of it all by this time and wanted to spend more quality time with Enrique and her grandchildren. Her priorities were changing. Her fashion business "worked for 25 years," Lilly told Koski, "but it wasn't going to work forever." So with a simple shrug of the shoulders, Lilly walked away from the world of fashion.

The same year that Lilly began to realize that her business was losing its luster and might eventually fall apart, her children's father, Peter Pulitzer, was making nasty headlines. On October 11, 1982, a *Time* magazine article titled "The Beautiful and the Damned" described one of the wildest high-society battles to go public in recent memory: Peter's attempt to dissolve his six-year marriage from his second wife, Roxanne, and gain custody of their five-year-old twin sons, McLean and Zachary (each named after a general, but just Mac and Zack in the daily headlines). News-papers around the country, especially the *New York Post*, followed every intimate revelation.

During the divorce and custody trial, held from September 20 to November 9, 1982, the people in Palm Beach (where the trial was held) mostly supported the fifty-three-year-old tycoon. Many in the media, however, championed the underdog, the

thirty-one-year-old Roxanne Renckens Dixon, a blue-eyed brunette cheerleader from the backwoods town of Cassadaga, New York, who clearly seemed to bask in the spotlight.

Every day, witnesses testified and brought up sordid details about the marriage. They named various men and women, well-known Palm Beach residents, with whom Roxanne had gone to bed during her marriage to Peter. There were charges of drug use, ménages à trois, incest, occult rituals, illegal transportation of cocaine from the Bahamas, and threats of murder. Peter ultimately won the custody battle, but he emerged looking not exactly like a model of wholesomeness himself.

Roxanne's titillating testimony about the couple's lovemaking and sexual paraphernalia as well as the goings-on in the mirror-walled bedroom of Peter's seventy-three-foot yacht was disturbing to most of the staid denizens of the resort, but particularly to Peter and Lilly's young adult son and their two daughters, who were only two, four, and five years younger than Roxanne. Lilly worried that the fallout from the overheated notoriety of the case would affect her children. Not much later, the children admitted in print that Lilly's own divorce from Peter had been traumatic for them.

After ninety-five hours of testimony, the case of *Pulitzer v. Pulitzer* concluded. According to the authors of *Palm Beach Babylon*, Murray Weiss and Bill Hoffmann, Peter and Roxanne,

> who had agreed on almost nothing during the court proceedings, both criticized press coverage as having been far too sensational. . . . The irony of their anger did not escape many of the two hundred reporters in attendance. It had been Pulitzer's grandfather, Joseph Pulitzer, who had made his fortune at the turn of the century splashing scandals and other people's misfortunes in giant headlines across his front pages. Perhaps the biblical promise

that the sins of the fathers shall be visited upon the sons unto the third generation had come true in the Pulitzer case.

One famous writer in attendance whose reports were particularly damning was Hunter S. Thompson. The eccentric gonzo journalist and author of the cult favorite *Fear and Loathing in Las Vegas*, who later wanted to end his life in Aspen by being shot out of a cannon, was covering the hearings for *Rolling Stone* magazine.

When Judge Carl H. Harper issued his final decision, Roxanne lost resoundingly. She was awarded forty-eight thousand dollars in "rehabilitative alimony" to be paid in installments of two thousand dollars a month, sixty thousand dollars' worth of jewelry, a twenty-thousand-dollar Porsche, and a seven-thousand-dollar cash equity in the couple's boat. Most devastating to Roxanne was the custody ruling regarding their two children. Peter received full custody of Mac and Zack, and Roxanne received only limited visitation rights.

Asked about one of the seamiest splits ever witnessed by Palm Beach society, Lilly replied to the *Sun Sentinel*'s Lorna Koski, "Roxanne just lived for the media. I guess Peter didn't care about his life being an open book because he wanted the kids. I think she had very bad advice, because she turned down a big sum of money and ended up with nothing."

Roxanne wrote an attention-getting book, *The Prize Pulitzer: The Scandal That Rocked Palm Beach* with Kathleen Maxa, about the fast-paced existence of the leisure class and her naive acceptance of her husband's excessive domination that pushed her to kinky sex. Her author's note began, "It wasn't easy establishing myself as Palm Beach's leading practitioner of 'gross moral misconduct,' to borrow a phrase from the court's final judgment in my divorce. I had a lot of competition. I also had a lot of help creating

this and other misconceptions about me, including that . . . untrue newspaper report that I slept with a trumpet."

But Roxanne proved to be resilient. After her tell-all book, she wrote three novels about Palm Beach. Three decades and several husbands later, according to a feature by Candace Jackson in the *Wall Street Journal* in 2011, Roxanne was ensconced in a twenty-three-thousand-square-foot, seven-bedroom rustic log-cabin-style mansion, set on three and a half acres among the San Miguel Mountains of Telluride, Colorado.

Her fifth husband, Tim Boberg, is the retired cofounder of a large management-consulting firm. After having exhausted all of their grown-up toys in the mansion—such as a built-in bowling alley, an indoor shooting range, a putting green, and an indoor lap pool with a waterfall—the couple put their house on the market in 2011 for $19.9 million.

Meanwhile, the consensus in Palm Beach is that Peter Pulitzer has been an exemplary and devoted father to Mac and Zack. Now grown-up men, they are officers of Pulitzer Groves Inc. and the Pulitzer Groves Packing Company in Okeechobee, Florida. Roxanne never lost touch with her sons. According to one New Yorker I spoke with who winters in Palm Beach, a couple of years ago when one of the periodic diseases that wipe out thousands of orange trees ran rampant in Florida's Indian River region, causing serious damage to the Pulitzer citrus groves, Roxanne and her deep-pocketed husband came to the rescue. They gave huge amounts of money to Mac and Zack in order for the brothers to replant and rescue the vegetation under their care. Peter and his third wife, Ingrid, seldom appear in Palm Beach. These days they prefer the seclusion of their home in the lovely citrus country north of the social buzz of Palm Beach, but the area is much more built up and residential today than it was when Peter was picking fruit and pruning his own orange trees in the snake-infested bramble.

The prize surname *Pulitzer*, the brand name on Lilly's contribution to fashion, had now fanned the disclosure of tawdry tidbits about Peter and Roxanne's lifestyle. This linkage never seems to have bothered Lilly. By the time Lilly quit working, she was more than ready to enjoy life with Enrique. She liked being Mrs. Rousseau. Although she had retained the Lilly Pulitzer label after divorcing Peter, from the moment she married Enrique she officially and insistently went by the name of Lilly Rousseau. One subject she doesn't hold back on is her second husband. "A wonderful, wonderful guy!" she told me.

The couple shared laughter and many tender moments together. Some years into their marriage, when the Rousseaus had just sold their house on Lake Worth, Enrique came upon an overgrown corner of the island, an estate that had long ago belonged to a family from St. Louis. The three crumbling structures on the 1.3-acre plot had pretty much been reclaimed by the jungle.

When Enrique showed the place to Lilly she said, "Oh, my God, we are going to have to build." She and Enrique fell instantly in love with the place. In Lilly's words, "It was a tropical oasis, really beautiful," with unusual specimens of trees—huge banyans, orange trees—and a little stream running through it. There were remnants of a Chinese garden with fruit trees, and unbelievably an old service road going through led right to the ocean. Lilly had remodeled houses before, but this time the two of them created something from scratch.

"No one else in oh-so-tasteful Palm Beach would dare put a house together like this," said Barbara Marshall in the *Palm Beach Post*. The nine bedrooms and eight bathrooms divided between the main house and the casita were planned to put up both Lilly's and Enrique's growing families, who often visited.

A bold L on the turquoise front door led through a terra-cotta foyer into a yellow living room the size of a ballroom. There were green-and-pink fabrics everywhere, and two huge refrigerators in the kitchen, where every Sunday both their offspring and various "visiting dignitaries," as Lilly called their friends, came together, as families traditionally do in Latin countries. The house was rather like the irrepressible couple who lived there: bursting with an exuberance of colors, treasured mementos and pedigreed antiques.

But tragedy soon appeared at Lilly's doorstep. Toward the end of the 1980s, Enrique was diagnosed with prostate cancer.

No strangers to personal sadness, in the past both the McKim and Phipps families had to take heart and to console each other in the face of illness. Because of Lilly's attachment to people in her inner circle, especially to members of her extended family—cousins, half-sister, step-brother, new wives, ex-husbands—and because she had always been emotionally tightly fastened to her two sisters, back in 1963 the sudden death of her beloved sister Memsie had nearly unhinged her. Marie Maude had played and integral part in getting Lilly's clothing enterprise off the ground. It was Marie Maude who had introduced her to former *Harper's Bazaar* fashion editor Laura Clarke, her savvy initial partner, and who had brought to Lilly's attention the colorful Key West silk-screened swatches from her future fabric design partners Peter Pell and Jimmy Russell. Heartbreakingly, Memsie had taken her own life after a series of hospitalizations for mental breakdowns in her twenties and at the end of a hurtful romantic relationship just before her thirty-third birthday.

Now, despite the bad news about Enrique's health, Lilly was filled with hope. She became completely devoted to caring for him, and they visited top doctors in New York. Enrique put up a brave five-year fight, but in 1993 he died in Lilly's arms. Lilly was devastated. A little later she herself suffered from

acute coronary problems and went through a serious operation at the Cleveland Clinic.

According to a childhood pal and Farmington classmate, while recovering from her heart bypass surgery, Lilly drove the doctors and nurses to the absolute limit. They simply couldn't cope with her stubbornness and determination to have things her way. They had a terrible time getting her to follow the doctors' orders. Her children were told she was the most difficult patient the world-famous clinic ever had.

For a brief period, those closest to Lilly were profoundly concerned about her. She had put on a lot of weight. She became remote, reclusive, and moody. She drank a little more than in the past, and at times she was quite difficult to be with.

CHAPTER 12

Lilly's Comeback

I N THE SPLENDID HOUSES ALONG THE SIXTEEN-MILE stretch of coastline that is Palm Beach, ever new attractive and achieving women—artists, producers, princesses, decorators, entrepreneurs, volunteers, matriarchs, and everyday moms, all integral to the mix that makes the island so unique—in time took over the limelight that Lilly once held. She was pleased.

Always rather shy by nature, she was by now tired and bothered by all the attention. A family-centered woman, she lavished her affectionate nature on her grandchildren and on all of the things growing in her enchanted jungle garden. Lilly made sure that the canopy of large banyan trees looming just beyond her house remained wild enough to accommodate nine cats, a dog, and a tortoise named Tortuga. With her house, Lilly created a sprawling world of upside-down bohemian charms and innate beauty that nourished the spirits and imaginations of all who came there.

Her company was put on hold for a decade. In the early 1990s, out of the blue, a group of smooth, fresh-faced, and style-conscious young Harvard MBAs—enamored all of their lives with Lilly's unique informal take on the good life—came calling. They were officially courting Lilly, in corporate parlance. Seeing the popularity of vintage Lillys among their friends and the way the garments were quickly scooped up whenever they appeared on eBay, they tried to convince her that it was time for the Lilly brand to have a renaissance.

The act of imagining a whole new generation—the friends of her children and grandchildren, a battalion of scrubbed, smiling young people in the colors of the rainbow and in amusing, swirling prints—charmed Lilly. She missed working with pretty colors, using her finely honed decorative instincts, and exercising her taste to make things that made others happy.

Yet it took some intense wooing on the part of the men who were putting together the business proposal before Lilly gave them the green light to revive the Lilly Pulitzer brand. She particularly liked the two good-looking and enthusiastic young men in charge of the group who visited her at home: James "Brad" Bradbeer Jr. and Scott A. Beaumont. They were working together at Eagle Eye Inc., an apparel company in New York, when they conceived the idea to revive the Lilly brand. After several more visits, they convinced Lilly to serve as a consultant to the new company, inspecting every new print and shape in order to decide whether they were authentically Lilly or not Lilly, but they told her that she needn't be involved in the firm's day-to-day activities.

Soon the printed clothes, with the help of a scrutinizing so-called pink-and-green police of preppy young socialites, took off once again. Now there were not only clothes designed for men, women, and children but also Lilly sheets, sunglasses, and fragrances. In the last dozen or so years, the company has been

doing more business than it did the first time around. In 2008, for instance, the company grossed a hundred million dollars.

The reborn Lillys inspired other designers such as Michael Kors, Oscar de la Renta and Cynthia Rowley, and were soon sported by such popular actresses as Ashley Judd and Renée Zellweger.

Positioned on a targeted-growth trajectory, Lilly (the brand) can be understood very easily as a successful relaunch. Every comeback story is unique. For unlike the specific ways that a brand like Halston or a designer like Diane von Furstenberg might opt to return to business, having the new Lillys in stores seemed, to Lilly, to be an organic step right back into the sunshine.

The focus in recent years of several large-scale retrospectives— particularly one at the Parsons School of Design in New York City and another at the Museum of Life Style and Design in Boynton Beach, Florida, called "For the Love of Lilly"—brought her a few cultural accolades that were long overdue.

It was essential that Lilly agree to play a consulting role in the company's new incarnation. For Bradbeer, the chairman of Sugartown Worldwide Inc., the company based in King of Prussia, Pennsylvania, that would own Lilly Pulitzer Inc. for seventeen years, and for Scott Beaumont, the CEO of the firm, meeting Lilly was "love at first sight," as Bradbeer was quoted in the *New Yorker*.

While both of them were working for Eagle Eye, they ran into a married couple so gung-ho on Lilly clothes and accessories that the two men quickly realized something: if they did not act right away on their instinctive certainty that the time was right to bring back Lilly, "somebody else who already had the same idea would beat us to it," Beaumont said. Bradbeer recalls, "You know, in life you sometimes think, God, I wish I'd thought of that, I wish I had done something about it." Bradbeer's mother wore Lillys and sold Lillys, first in Bryn Mawr, Pennsylvania, then in La Jolla, California. His first recollection as a child was grabbing his mother, her floral-printed shift, and the little white bows on the shift.

Beaumont, slim and tall like Bradbeer, likes to talk about his experiences in what it takes to bring a brand back. It seldom succeeds in the novelty-hungry world of fashion. The company's namesake, of course, provided him with plenty of material for a promotable back story. Above all, the business partners recognized a niche. According to Beaumont, "We saw that the country was . . . getting older and richer and was moving to the beach. If you define the Great Lakes as a beach—and many people who live there do—seventy-five percent of the U.S. population lives within a ninety-minute drive to the beach, and eighty-five percent of vacations involve going to the beach." This was the beginning of the vision of targeting and strengthening the Lilly brand.

With the renewed health and vigor of Lilly Pulitzer Inc., by December 2010 it was only a matter of time before another suitor would come knocking with an offer to expand and diversify the company. So Bradbeer and Beaumont, two preppy gentlemen, decided to accept the offer of Oxford Industries to acquire the Lilly Pulitzer brand. This acquisition seemed to be a good fit for everyone concerned, and it also arrived at a good moment. For young families today, there is a need for easy, economical clothing.

Based in Atlanta, Oxford Industries is an international apparel company with a diverse portfolio of holdings, including Kenneth Cole, Dockers, and Geoffrey Beene; its channel of distribution is so varied and expansive that it will more than likely ensure new articulations of the Lilly Pulitzer aesthetic.

"As we got to know each other, we quickly realized that there is an excellent strategic and cultural fit," Oxford's, Thomas Caldecott Chubb III, said. According to the *New York Times*, under the deal Oxford paid $60 million in cash to Sugartown Worldwide and will pay up to $20 million more in additional sums if the

clothier hits certain earning targets. Beaumont and Bradbeer continue to run the company as a unit of Oxford.

In a 2008 speech Beaumont stated that Pulitzer's core customer is "twenty-five to forty, with a household income of two hundred thousand dollars or up, well educated, travels a lot, social life is based around the home." The company breaks down the base into three groups: chic elite, suburban belles, and aspiring customers. "The key with positioning," he said, "is that you have to have the courage to target, which means there will be a whole lot of people you can't sell to." That is what the company has succeeded in doing ever since the first orange juice stand: creating the perfect niche and then cornering that market.

Lilly's kind of comeback success almost never happens in the fashion industry. Despite the publicity and backing of actress Sarah Jessica Parker and Hollywood mogul Harvey Weinstein, the attempt to revive Halston fell flat on its face in the autumn of 2011. After the British designer Laura Ashley's premature death, her family tried to bring back her daintily flowered longish English garden dresses but soon found that the prints sold better as wallpaper and decorator fabrics and stopped making the clothes. Though her wrap dress of the 1970s did make a comeback decades later, Diane von Furstenberg made sure that her high profile in the fashionable world was never out of the limelight. The closest comparison to Lilly Pulitzer is Coco Chanel, who closed down her Paris atelier, then revived it successfully with the brand going on and on, potentially forever.

Not without tumult since its inception, the Lilly Pulitzer brand now seems to be on a steady course. The firm keeps expanding, with Dan River doing the Lilly bedding and Pulse Points doing the licensing of Pulitzer fragrances. Early in the new millennium Lilly added stationery and appointment books for the Party Animal and co-wrote two Essentially Lilly books on festive entertaining. All of these have sold well in her clothing boutiques and department stores. Now, through Oxford Industries' larger

corporate framework, these new products and the familiar dres-
ses and colors are reaching more households than ever before.

Despite her deserved fame and grande-dame status, Lilly has
remained a surprisingly natural and unaffected person. She jokingly
calls herself the Queen of the Jungle. A true survivor, she is both
comfortable and comforting. She has often told her friends, "I love
my children more than life itself!" Today the three— Peter Jr., who
lives in the Pacific Northwest, and Floridians Minnie McCluskey and
Liza Calhoun—all regularly gather around her with their spouses
and their children, Lilly's eight grandchildren. "What has mattered
to Lilly the most all her life," said Edwina Millington, "is her family."
She still loves cooking huge amounts of interesting dishes for a
crowd "expando-style," as she puts it. Her wit and one-liners are as
sharp and delightful as ever.

Even her daughters' ex-husbands—fathers of Minnie's chil-
dren Rodman and Lilly Leas and of Liza's sons Chris and Bobby
Leidy—are welcome in what Lilly likes to refer to as her jungle—
her superbly decorated Palm Beach house, encapsulating the
pleasurably informal life she has created for herself with bright
floral prints and big cozy pillows strewn everywhere. It is sur-
rounded by a wild grove of coconut palms, banana and grapefruit
trees, orchids, gardenias, jasmine, and hibiscus—a magical acre
where she spends most of her days.

At eighty, she no longer looks exotic. She has colored her hair
blond, and she wears it in a conservative short pageboy, which is
becoming but is a total change from the Gauguin Polynesian
princess look of her youth. "I find gray hair depressing," she says.

Somewhat self-effacingly, she quips about the Lilly as "just a
lovely little thing that was part of everyone's life."

She harbors no resentment toward today's more glitzy Palm
Beach and the latest big-bucks names from the top of the Forbes

400 list like David Koch, Stephen Schwarzman, Wilbur Ross, and Vera Wang building extraordinary new beachfront villas and buying up the legendary Mizner and Fatio villas. She surrounds herself with old friends and her sister Flossie, who winters in Palm Beach, comes over every day to see her. Although Lilly stays away from the resort's frantic high-season social scene, she is alive to the pulse of a new young generation that lives and works and raises its children there and is concerned about the cost of it all. Her life seems balanced, enriched by a sense of propriety and generosity.

Lilly still never worries about what other people think, and she does as she pleases. She remains a rare bird of paradise and continues to live according to her individualistic impulses, a lover of pleasure and of people who love pleasure.

According to Diana Vreeland, the iconic former *Vogue* editor, the definition of an original is "the energy of imagination, deliberation, and invention, which fall into a natural rhythm totally one's own, maintained by innate discipline and a keen sense of pleasure—these are the ingredients of style. And all who have it share one thing: originality."

At a key moment in her life, Lilly Pulitzer accomplished nothing less than giving form to her own original self—an endangered creature rather like some of the birds and flowering plants of the Florida tropics all about her.

Lilly is a woman who is making something. The countless ways through which Lilly has been able to make herself felt in the world are rare and most original.

Source Notes

My most significant source for the writing of *Lilly* was a quarter-century of intermittent visits to Palm Beach. It was through these visits that I met Lilly Rousseau, as she preferred to be called then. While researching this book during the last two years, there were also several cordial but more cautious telephone conversations between us. Being able to see her in action, being able to hear her voice, her laugh, her inflections, her inimitable way of tossing back tart one-liners that were both hilarious and right on the beam, gave me a sense of the woman that added aspects of her personality and emotional depth, which otherwise would have been missing from my story of her life.

1. It Girl of the Sixties

Perhaps the most balanced and astutely observed volume for my research of life in Palm Beach during the sixties was *Palm Beach: The Place, the People, Its Pleasures and Palaces* by John Ney (Boston:

Little, Brown & Co.,1966), a compelling and highly readable book on the Kennedy era at the resort, replete with details about the activities of the newly elected young president, the town's attitude to rising design star Lilly Pulitzer, and stories about the Phipps family, especially Michael Phipps. Invaluable for an overview of Pulitzer's style contributions were John Fairchild predicting in *The Fashionable Savages* (Garden City, New York: Doubleday, 1965) the future goldmine and phenomenon of Lilly's shifts; Eleanor Lambert describing the garment's evolution from "a snob uniform, then a general fashion craze" in *The World of Fashion: People, Places, Resources* (New York: R.R. Bowker, 1976); and Marylin Bender recognizing the impact of the aristocratic aura Jacqueline Kennedy and Lilly Pulitzer brought to mass-produced fashion as role models in *The Beautiful People* (New York: Coward-McCann, 1967). Todd S. Purdum's feature story on the Kennedy inauguration in *Vanity Fair* in February 2011 and a description of the fashions at the various celebrative gatherings around the inauguration appearing in the *Washington Post* on January 22, 1961, were highly informative in helping to catch the hopeful spirit of the new presidency. John Ney's verbal anecdote about young mothers all wearing Lillys on the grounds of the Palm Beach Day School was supplemented for me by one short amateur film of the school children in action on the Sea View Avenue sports field at a friend's private screening. A generous and incisive personal interview with Palm Beach–bred Tiffany executive Fernanda Kellogg provided me with some invaluable insights into the resort's youth quake during the sixties as well as the marvelous "It Girl" quote about Lilly. Some perceptive data and original interpretation of the childlike play dresses that characterize Lilly's fashions, as well as the quoted advice from Lilly's doctor were gleaned from Larissa MacFarquhar's article "Everything Lilly" in the *New Yorker*, September 4, 2000. A variety of perspectives on Lilly, her life style, her fabrics,

and her silhouettes were provided by "Beachy Keen . . . Lilly Pulitzer Rousseau Enjoys a Second Blossoming" in *People*, September 4, 2000; and "Textile Briefs in *HFN* (the weekly newspaper for the Home Furnishing Network), February 28, 2000. "Light, Color, Action! The Joyful Florida House of Lilly Pulitzer," *Vogue*, January 1975; "Barefoot Tycoon Makes Lillies Bloom All Over" *Life*, February 8, 1968; and a special edition of *Palm Beach Life* "Vintage Glossy 1968" with Lilly and Peter Pulitzer sailing away on its cover helped fill in some of the missing pieces about the couple's special way of life.

2. The Healing Properties of Florida Orange Juice

Lilly's nervous collapse soon after the birth of her third child and her hospitalization in Westchester County in New York have been covered by a multiplicity of magazine articles. Although some of the sources contain conflicting information (especially about the number of months she spent away in treatment and the precise manifestations of her symptoms), they, along with insightful more recent profiles of the designer, were invaluable as I researched this chapter. I'm particularly indebted to *W* magazine writer Lorna Koski's in-depth interviews with Lilly: "The Return of Lilly" in *W*, October 1993, and " A Former Palm Beach Fashion Queen Makes a Colorful Comeback with More Flair Than Ever" in the January 1994 South Florida *Sun Sentinel*. Koski elicits some of the most candid and reflective quotes from Lilly, such as "My marriage was driving me crazy . . . and I did not want to admit that even to myself." And that after months of counseling "I became much more assertive," plus starting her business with her station wagon, driving up the back entrances of mansions that she was used to going in the front door, she "got to know every cook, every butler in Palm beach." In Laura Jacobs's widely researched and richly drawn *Vanity Fair* portrait, "Palm Beach's

Barefoot Princess" from July 2003, the writer alludes to friends noticing Lilly still being somewhat quiet when she returned to Florida after her illness and Lilly blaming herself for jumping into marriage while still immature: "It was just my next adventure." Larissa MacFarquhar's trenchant September 4, 2000, "Annals of Fashion" piece on Lilly in the *New Yorker* probes how Lilly felt being in a psychiatric clinic and includes the quote "I had a great time . . . like boarding school, very regimented." All three of the above writers quote the doctor as prescribing work to be an antidote to Lilly's feeling blue. All three remark on Lilly's unconventional work choices, first in Appalachia, then selling oranges in Palm Beach. Illuminating details about Lilly's activities in the hinterlands of eastern Kentucky came from records kept by the mule courier program and midwifery center as well as the writings of the late pioneer of maternal care, Mary Breckenridge, from the Frontier Nursing Service in Wendover, Kentucky. While Lilly seldom complains and never utters an unkind word about Florida, in her *Essentially Lilly Guide to Colorful Entertaining* (New York: HarperCollins, 2004) she admits to coauthor Jay Mulvaney that back when she first moved to Palm Beach summers in the lively winter resort were "D-E-A-D." I consulted references in the book *The Noonday Demon* by Andrew Solomon (New York: Simon & Schuster, 2001) and recent reports from the Mayo Clinic regarding postpartum depression. Information from the Indian River Citrus League helped document the history of Florida oranges and the laws governing their harvesting and sale.

3. Barefoot on Worth Avenue

Beyond the three extensive, thought-provoking recent profiles by *Vanity Fair*'s Laura Jacobs, *W*'s Lorna Koski, and the *New Yorker*'s Larissa MacFarquhar, the following articles helped chart Lilly's trajectory from curbside orange juicer to fashion designer:

"Fashion: The Lilly," *Time*, June 1, 1962, and Linda Marx, "No One Needs to be Shiftless This Summer, Thanks to Lilly Pulitzer," *People*, 1982. *Halcyon Days: An American Family through Three Generations* by Peggie Phipps Boegner and Richard Gachot (New York: Old Westbury Gardens and Harry N. Abrams, Inc. 1986) was indispensable in tracing the history of the steel industry and one of its publicity-shy self-made giants. The book, based on Phipps family letters and rarely seen personal photographs of Phipps descendants in pursuit of field sports, exotic travel, and elegant family celebrations at their houses on Long Island and in Palm Beach and compiled and written by founder Henry Phipps Jr.'s granddaughter and a Long Island neighbor, was an indispensable guide to the rarefied sphere of style and taste that surrounded and inspired Lilly since childhood. Two books also useful to understanding the life and times of Pittsburgh's post–Civil War industrial millionaires were *The Autobiography of Andrew Carnegie* (Boston: Houghton Mifflin, 1920) and *Henry Clay Frick: An Intimate Portrait* by Martha Frick Symington Sanger (New York: Abbeville Press, 1998).

4. Rich, Richer, Richest

The following books helped immensely in supplying the background story of Lilly's parents: *Triumvirate McKim, Meade & White: Art, Architecture, Scandal in America's Gilded Age* by Mosette Broderick (New York: Alfred A. Knopf, 2010); *A Monograph of McKim, Meade & White*: 1879–1915 (New York Architectural Book Publishing, 1915); and Michael M. Mooney's biography *Evelyn Nesbitt and Stanford White* (New York: William Morrow, 1976). I researched the archival holdings of the New York Public Library including *The McKim Descendants of James McKim*, vol. B and the Maloney Collection of McKim-Garrison Family papers, ca. 1814–1940; this research also consisted of the

personal papers of Charles Folen McKim, which led to the Folen branch of the family and their involvement with abolitionist John Brown. Lillian Bostwick's father, Jabez A. Bostwick, one of the founding partners of the Standard Oil Company, made many headlines. Most famous of these was his dramatic death by a fire reported in an article in the *New York Times* on August 18, 1892. As for the vast fortune left by his widow, the article dealing with her famous gem collection, "$29,264,181 to Heirs of Mrs. Bostwick," appeared in the *New York Times* on November 5, 1921. The family legacy of participation in the fields of horses and aviation has been chronicled by innumerable thoroughbred racing journals such as the *Daily Telegraph* and the *Daily Racing Form* as well as the archives of the Aiken Thoroughbred Racing Hall of Fame, the Museum of Polo and Hall of Fame, and the United States Museum of Racing and Hall of Fame. Especially useful was a *Time* magazine article from June 27, 1932, "Gentleman Jockey," about G. H. "Pete" Bostwick, and the obituary of Dunbar W. Bostwick that appeared in the *New York Times* on January 29, 2006.

5. Horse Country

An article appearing in *Quest* magazine in 1990, "The Phipps Family" chronicled the marriages of characters in this chapter. It showed that the sportive Harvard- and Yale-educated Phipps men also chose physically stunning and stylish women, who became pacesetters, including C. Z. Guest. In February 1973, *Town & Country* magazine did a ten-page photo essay on the Phipps women a few years after the family opened more areas of their once private Old Westbury Gardens in New York to the public. Most helpful to this facet of Lilly's story were several illuminating interviews I had with the great-granddaughter of Henry Phipps Jr., Dita Naylor-Leyland, who was for many

years a resident of Palm Beach and who underlined some of the interesting generational shifts. The influence of horseback riding on Lilly's childhood is mentioned in two of Lilly's own lifestyle books and in personal interviews I had with several of her fellow equestriennes on Long Island, including distant cousin Patricia Montgomerie. Concerning the Phipps family and their unique prominence in the breeding and racing of thoroughbred horses, Whitney Tower's February 22, 1965 article in *Sports Illustrated*, "Bold Is the Badge of Champions," offered a knowledgeable insider's study of the unmatched successes of Gladys Mills Phipps and her son Ogden Phipps, the owners and breeders of the legendary thoroughbred sire Bold Ruler, whose offspring included Secretariat. Over the years the late Whitney Tower was a friend and colleague who shared his knowledge of the history of the sport of kings, consulting with me several times and lending his seasoned perspective for *Town & Country*'s then annual guide to horse-country happenings. Extremely useful for information on the Phipps real estate holdings, especially regarding the development of Sutton Place and the splendor of Mrs. Frederick E. Guest's penthouse, was *New York, New York: How the Apartment House Transformed the Life of the City* by Elizabeth Hawes (New York: Alfred A, Knopf, 1993). How the world of polo inspires contemporary status accessories and weekend clothing worldwide today was examined by the *Financial Times* on July 24, 2010, in two articles: "Sport Gives Life to Global Fashion Empire" by Nicola Copping and "To Enter Polo's Top Ranks, Just Pay the Fee" by Jenny MacArthur. Among the *New York Times* articles consulted for this section were: "C. Z. Guest, Beauty Who Rose to New York Society" by Enid Nemy, which appeared on November 10, 2003, and the *Times*'s obituaries of Mrs. Michael Phipps of Palm Beach; Hubert B. Phipps, publisher of the *Livestock Breeder Journal* in Warrenton, Virginia; and the Honorable Mrs. Frederick E. Guest, the former Amy Phipps.

6. Of Preps and Debs

Essential reading reflecting on Lilly's prep school experience included: *Miss Porter's School: A History* by Barbara Donohue and Nancy Davis (New Haven, CT: Northeast Graphics, 1992); *When I Was at Farmington* by Abby Farwell Ferry (Chicago: Ralph Fletcher Seymour, 1931); "The Code of Miss Porters" by Evgenia Peretz in *Vanity Fair*, July 2009; *Reading Jackie: Her Autobiography in Books* by William Kuhn (New York: Nan A. Talese/Doubleday, 2010); and *Sister: The Life of Legendary Interior Decorator, Mrs. Parrish II* by Apple Parrish Bartlett and Susan Bartlett Crater (New York: St Martin's Press, 2000). Various newspaper society-page features from the *New York Times* I consulted about Lilly and her sisters' coming out parties include: "Cotillion Will Assist Infirmary," September 14, 1947; "Tea Dance Will Aid Botanical Garden," December 14, 1947," and "Debutantes Feted at Christmas Ball: 130 Young Women Honored," December 23, 1947. Some personal interviews I conducted with girlhood friends and Miss Porter's School classmates of Lilly's yielded the insightful and witty remembrances of Edwina Millington as well as shared prep school memories from Alexander (Sandy) McLanahan. I also had memorable conversations with former magazine colleague Polly Mellen and once-upon-a-time Farmington student and *Town & Country* contributor, the late Peggy Bedford Bancroft d'Arenberg d'Uzes.

7. Falling in Love with a Pulitzer

Some notable sources for this chapter were two outstanding biographies: *Pulitzer: A Life in Politics, Print, and Power* by James McGrath Morris (New York: Harper, 2010), and *Pulitzer: A Life* by Dennis Brian (New York: John Wiley & Sons, 2001). I also consulted the following: an article from the *New York Social Diary* by Clemmer Mayhew, "Impressive Woman: Gladys Pulitzer Preston,

Patsy to her Friends," November 4, 2011; "The World's Loveliest Sportswomen," *Sports Illustrated*, December 25, 1961; "Lewis Thompson Preston, Eighth President of the World Bank Group, 1991–1995," published by the World Bank Group in 2010; "House of Munn: The Palm Beach Story" by Augustus C. Mayhew (November 24, 2006) in the *New York Social Diary*; and "The Munn Family: Being a Record of the Descendants of Benjamin Munn through Stephen Ball Munn of the Fifth Generation" by William Frederick Cornell (New York: New York Public Library, 1941). I also conducted several interviews with Pulitzer relatives and friends of the family.

8. Lillys Blooming Everywhere

Along with the previously mentioned articles by Jacobs, Koski, MacFarquhar, and Marx, Sarah Haight wrote vividly about how Lilly created a viable business in "Lilly Land" in *W*, December 2008. Newspaper sources included "Key West Hand Print Fabrics" in the *St. Petersburg Times*, February 13, 1968; "Lilly's Latest Boutique" in the *Sarasota Herald Tribune*, November 14, 1963; and "Palm Beach Woman Injured in Crash" in the *Palm Beach Daily News*, May 15, 1964, which shed light on the Lilly Pulitzer label's expansion and growing recognition. The Gallery at Green Street in Key West was helpful with information about textile artist Suzie Depoo-Zuzek. I also consulted the widespread blogging regarding vintage Lillys and their labels. Offering considerable texture and atmosphere to this chapter were my interviews with fashion editors June Weir and Eve Hatch Holmes and Slim Aarons's books *A Wonderful Time*, (New York: Harper & Row, 1984), *Once Upon A Time* (New York: Harry N. Abrams Inc., 2003), *A Place in the Sun* (New York: Harry N. Abrams, 2005), and *Poolside with Slim Aarons* (New York: Harry N. Abrams, 2007). The work of another visual chronicler of the world's celebrated playgrounds,

Stolen Moments: The Photographs of Ronny Jaques by Pamela Fiori (New York: Glitterati Inc., 2008), includes a particularly revealing portrait of newlyweds Peter and Lilly with their pet monkey. *Life* photographer Howell Conant, Grace Kelly's favorite photographer, and several respected South Florida photographers, Bob Davidoff, Bert Morgan, and Mort Kaye, also captured inspiring images of the Pulitzers at both work and play.

9. The Perpetual Party Town

I browsed through sources covering decades of charity events: the *Palm Beach Shiny Sheet*; Aileen Mehle's "Suzy" columns in *W*; Eugenia Sheppard's fashion/society columns in the *Herald Tribune*; issues of *Vogue* from the 1920s, *Quest*, and *Avenue*; and Who's Who lists. I also consulted "Palm Beach: The Greatest Little Beach Town on Earth," a twenty-page article in *Town & Country*, March 1983; "Pucci's Jet-Set Revolution by Amy Fine Collins, *Vanity Fair*, October 2000; and "Made in Miami: The Development of the Sportswear Industry in Florida 1900–1960," *Journal of Social History*, September 22, 2007. I consulted books including *"Splash! A History of Swimwear* by Richard Martin and Harold Koda (New York: Rizzoli International, 1990); *Making Waves: Swimsuits and the Undressing of America* (San Francisco: Chronicle Books, 1989); *Emilio Pucci* by Mariuccia Casadio (New York: Assouline, 2003); *Women's Bathing and Swimming Costume in the United States* (Washington, D.C: Smithsonian Institution Press, 1968); *The Palm Beach Sketchbook* by Bill Olendorf, text by Agnes Ash (Northfield, IL: Olendorf, 1988), *Palm Beach: An Architectural Legacy* by Polly Earl (New York: Rizzoli, 1992); *Henry Flagler: The Astonishing Life and Times of the Visionary Robber Baron Who Founded Florida* by David Chandler (New York: Macmillan, 1986); *A Capitalist Romance; Singer and the Sewing Machine* by Ruth Brandon (Philadelphia: J.B. Lippincott Co., 1977); *Heiress: The*

Rich Life of Marjorie Merriweather Post by William Wright (New York: New Republic Books, 1978); and *Wicked Palm Beach* by Eliott Kleinberg (Charleston, SC: History Press. 2009).

10. Lilly's New Love

Books I found indispensable were: *The Sugar King of Havana: The Rise and Fall of Julio Lobo, Cuba's Last Tycoon* by John Paul Rathbone (New York: Penguin Press 2010); *Great Houses of Havana, A Century of Cuban Style* (New York: Monacelli Press, 2011); and *Cubanismo! The Vintage Book of Contemporary Cuban Literature* edited and with an introduction by Cristina Garcia (New York: Vintage Books, May 2003). Magazine articles that were helpful included: "Cuba That American Rum and Rumba Tourists Never Saw" and "A Day in the Life of Havana Glamour Girl Alina Johnson Aguilera," *Life*, February 1950; "All Havana Broke Loose: An Oral History of Tropicana" by Jean Stein, *Vanity Fair*, September 2011; "Hearts, Flowers and True Love: A Palm Beach Wedding Diary" by Augustus Mayhew, *New York Social Diary*, February 15, 2011; and "The Battle Rages in Media and Congress Over Everglades Sugar," *Knight Ridder/Tribune*, October 27, 1999. I also conducted personal interviews with Kirk Henckels, Margarita Barrera of New York, and Gonzalo Garcia-Pedroso of Miami, among others.

11. The Stormy Season

These were some helpful books as I researched this chapter: *The Prize Pulitzer* by Roxanne Pulitzer with Kathleen Maxa (New York: Villard Books, 1987), and *Palm Beach Babylon* by Murray Weis and Bill Hoffmann (New York: Birch Lane Press, 1992). Articles I used as sources include: "The Beautiful and the Damned" by Kurt Andersen and Marilyn Alva, *Time*, October 11, 1982; Pulitzer's

Plea: Publishing Heir Begs for Custody of Children by Tim Palleson, *Washington Post*, October 6, 1982; "Pulitzer," Richard Cohen's column in the *Washington Post*, January 9, 1983; "The Mansion of Grown-Up Toys by Candace Jackson, *Wall Street Journal*, August 5, 2011; "Lilly Pulitzer Inc.'s Chapter 11 Bankruptcy Filing" by Pamela G, Hollie, *New York Times*, November 30, 1984; and "Lilly Pulitzer, Inc. Makes Bankruptcy-Law Filing," *Wall Street Journal* Western edition, November 29, 1984.

12. Lilly's Comeback

These newspapers had helpful coverage of the massive relaunch of the Lilly brand and museum exhibits of Lilly Pulitzer designs: "Fun Designs Make Lilly a Winner," *New York Post*, September 22, 2002; "Lilly, 50, Hasn't Aged a Day" by Eric Wilson, *New York Times* November 6, 2008; "Cooling Off in Short Dresses" by Anne-Marie Schiro, *New York Times*, July 23, 1996; and "The Pink-and-Green Police . . ." by Monique P. Yazigi, *New York Times*, May 17, 1998. Other useful print sources included: "Letter from Palm Beach: Talking Fashion" by William Norwich, *Vogue*, February 1994; "WWD Forum: Building a Better Brand," Scott Beaumont, executive officer of Lilly Pulitzer, Inc., on what it takes to bring back a brand, *Women's Wear Daily*, October 4, 2006; "Lilly Pulitzer Grows Up with Dan River" by Brent Felgner, *Home Textiles Today*, February 26, 2007; "Prep Stays Hot as Lilly Pulitzer Is Sold for $60 Million" by Michael J. de la Merced, *New York Times*, December 21, 2010; and "It's Preppy Prints at Pulitzer Party" by Marshall Heyman, *Wall Street Journal*, January 5, 2011;. Finally, the splendid book *Diana Vreeland: DV* (New York: Alfred A Knopf, 1984) gave wonderful insights into the fashion world.

Photo Credits

Frontispiece, pp. 101, 106 (bottom), Historical Society of Palm Beach County; pp. 95, 97, Howell Conant/Bob Adelman Books, Inc.; pp. 96, 98, 99 (top), 100, Lorna Drake, Freudy Photos Archives, LLC; pp. 99 (bottom), 103 (top), 104, 109, 110 (top right), Slim Aarons/Getty Images; p. 102, Cecil Stoughton/John F. Kennedy Presidential Library; pp. 103 (bottom), 105, 107 (bottom), Bert Morgan Archive; p. 106 (top), Alfred Eisenstaedt/Getty Images; p. 107 (top), Bert Morgan/Getty Images; p. 108, Courtesy Old Westbury Gardens; p. 110 (top left), New York Public Library; p. 110 (bottom), Courtesy private family archives; pp. 111, 112 (bottom), 113, (top), Davidoff Studios, Palm Beach, FL; p. 112 (top), Nina Leen/Getty Images; p. 113 (bottom), ©WWD/Condé Nast/Corbis; p. 114 (top), Diana Walker/Getty Images; p. 114 (bottom), Jennifer Graylock/AP.

Index

Page numbers in *italics* indicate illustrations.

Bostwick, Albert C., 44
Bostwick, Albert, Jr., 45
Bostwick, Dorothy, 47
Bostwick, Dunbar, 46, *106*
Bostwick, Evelyn, 44
Bostwick, George Herbert (Pete), 45–46, 65, *106*
Bostwick, Helen C., 44–45
Bostwick, Jabez A., 43–44
Bostwick, Laura Curtis, *106*
Bostwick, Lillian Stokes, 43, 44, 45, 46. *See also* McKim, Lillian; Phipps, Lillian
Bostwick Field, 46, *106*
boutiques
 of Lilly, *97*, 142–143, 154–155, 200
 in Palm Beach, 178, 189
Bradbeer, James, Jr., *113*, 212, 213, 214
Brady, Beverly, 92
Brady, Kitty Douglas, 87
Brady, Nicholas F., 87, 92
Breakers Hotel, 163, 166
Breckinridge, Mary, 17–18, 19
Brian, Denis, 127, 128–129
Brisbane, Arthur, 126
Burke, Billie, 131
business
 boutiques, *97*, 142–143, 154–155, 200
 citrus sales, 20, 21
 decision to pursue, 16
 fashion industry and, 199–200
 first dress sales, 37
 gift box/basket sales, 21, 142, 155

having fun with, 150–151, 152
"little nothing" dresses and, 137–139
orange juice stand, 21, 25–26, 35, 137
sewing factory, 146
turning dresses into full-time, 141–145
Via Mizner shop, *97*, 142–143, 154
See also Lilly Pulitzer Inc.

Calhoun, Liza Pulitzer. *See* Pulitzer, Liza
Cameron, Alexander, *103*
Carnegie, Andrew, 29, 30–31, 32, 33
Carnegie, Phipps, 31
Carnegie Steel Company, 31–32, 33
Carstairs, Albert, 44
Carstairs, Betty, 47
Cartier and polo, 66
Casa Bendita, 26–27
Cassini, Oleg, 140
Chandler, David Leon, 163
Chanel, Coco, 215
Chapin School, Manhattan, 78, 80
Chavchavadze, David, 118
Chubb, Thomas Caldecott, III, 214
citrus sales, 20, 21
Clark, Edward, 53
Clark, F. Ambrose, 52–53
Clark, Laura. *See* Robbins, Laura Pyzel
Clark, Sterling, 52–53
Clarke, Laura, 206
Clemente, Deirdre, 163